AIRDRIE

Unicorns

by William Dudley

ReferencePoint Press™

San Diego, CA

©2008 ReferencePoint Press, Inc.

For more information, contact
ReferencePoint Press, Inc.
PO Box 27779
San Diego, CA 92198
www.ReferencePointPress.com

Picture credits:
Cover: Dreamstime
AP/Wide World Photos, 82
Dreamstime, 6, 7, 8, 51, 91
Fortean Picture Archive, 29, 35, 65, 87
North Wind, 21, 44, 61, 67, 83, 89
Photos.com, 85
Science Photo Library, 56, 72
Wikipedia, 42
The Yorch Project, 11

Series design and book layout:
Amy Stirnkorb

LIBRARY OF CONGRESS CATALOGING-IN-PUBLICATION DATA

Dudley, William, 1964-
Unicorns / William Dudley.
   p. cm. -- (Mysterious & unknown)
ISBN-13: 978-1-60152-028-9 (hardback)
ISBN-10: 1-60152-028-X (hardback)
1. Unicorns--Juvenile literature. I. Title.
GR830.U6D83 2008
398.24'54--dc22

                                                                                    2007011805

CONTENTS

FOREWORD

"Strange is our situation here upon earth."
—*Albert Einstein*

Since the beginning of recorded history, people have been perplexed, fascinated, and even terrified by events that defy explanation. While science has demystified many of these events, such as volcanic eruptions and lunar eclipses, some remain outside the scope of the provable. Do UFOs exist? Are people abducted by aliens? Can some people see into the future? These questions and many more continue to puzzle, intrigue, and confound despite the enormous advances of modern science and technology.

It is these questions, phenomena, and oddities that Reference-Point Press's *The Mysterious & Unknown* series is committed to exploring. Each volume examines historical and anecdotal evidence as well as the most recent theories surrounding the topic in debate. Fascinating primary source quotes from scientists, experts, and eyewitnesses as well as in-depth sidebars further inform the text. Full-color illustrations and photos add to each book's visual appeal. Finally, source notes, a bibliography, and a thorough index provide further reference and research support. Whether for research or the curious reader, *The Mysterious & Unknown* series is certain to satisfy those fascinated by the unexplained.

INTRODUCTION

Wrapped in Mystery

"If God had not created the Unicorn, man would have invented him, for he has a form and nature that must exist."
—Welleran Poltarnees, *A Book of Unicorns.*

For thousands of years people have been fascinated and charmed by the unicorn. It is, at first glance, easy to describe and easy to find. A unicorn is a mythical horse with a single horn in its forehead. The word itself comes from the Latin word *unicornis,* meaning "one horn." Unicorns can be found in the toy departments of stores or as decorations in children's rooms. They can be found in calendars and posters—white horses, glowing in the moonlight, their flashing horns giving a fleeting glimpse of a world of fairies and magic. They can be found in store windows and entrances, as decorative signs or as figurines made of china,

A unicorn is a mythical horse with a single horn in its forehead. This poster shows a unicorn with its foal.

pewter, plastic, or glass. They can be found in art museums, in tapestries, paintings, and sculptures. They can be found in popular fantasy novels. A beautiful unicorn plays a tragically pivotal role in J.K. Rowling's *Harry Potter and the Sorcerer's Stone:* Its blood keeps the evil Lord Voldemort alive. Jewel, a noble warrior unicorn, is the best friend of the last king of Narnia in *The Last Battle* by C.S. Lewis. Jill, another character in that book, falls in love with Jewel much in the same way that people have fallen in

love with unicorns in general. Lewis writes: "She thought—and she wasn't far wrong—that he was the shiningest, delicatest, most graceful animal she had ever met: and he was so gentle and soft of speech that, if you hadn't known, you would hardly have believed how fierce and terrible he could be in battle."[1]

Gentle and delicate—yet fierce and terrible in battle. This seeming paradox is one of many mysteries surrounding this animal. Indeed, the more one reads and learns about the unicorn, the

Unicorns are found in lots of literature and fantasy writings. This computer-generated unicorn is seen with its master.

more complex and mysterious it becomes. Instead of a single-horned horse, literary and artistic unicorn descriptions have featured tiny goats, large asses with three-colored horns, creatures as huge as mountains, and animals with various combinations of traits from other beasts, including elephants, antelopes, oxen, and deer. Instead of myth, the unicorn has been considered a zoological fact by many people, educated and uneducated, for much of human history. Books were written to defend its existence and to describe sightings in remote parts of Africa, Asia, and other parts of the world. Doctors and pharmacists sold its horn as a miracle cure. Instead of cute toys and pictures, unicorns have been important symbols in religion and art. Yet, throughout all the differing versions, settings, and stories of unicorns, the animal's nobility and goodness has remained a constant fixture.

The unicorn remains wrapped in mystery. For many centuries, the central question surrounding the unicorn was whether it really existed. Today the mystery is more about why so many people believed in unicorns, and why these mythical beasts have had such a hold on the human imagination.

CHAPTER 1

Ancient Stories and Images

Unicorns, it is said, reside in deep, dark forests, remote deserts, mountain peaks, or other places away from humans. But an excellent place to spot a unicorn today is in a transplanted medieval complex in New York City.

There, in a 4-acre park (1.6ha) overlooking the Hudson River, a short subway or bus ride from the skyscrapers and the hustle and bustle of Broadway, Times Square, and Wall Street, one can find the Cloisters. A cloister is a medieval-era architectural feature consisting of four roofed or vaulted passageways enclosing a square or rectangular open courtyard—thus creating interior places for gardens and hallways that are open to the air but sheltered from the rain and snow. The Cloisters is a complex built in the 1930s that includes parts of 5-centuries-old cloisters that were actually disassembled from monasteries and other buildings in France and transported to and reassembled in New York. Since

This tapestry, titled The Lady and the Unicorn, *was made in the fifteenth century in Paris. It shows a maiden who has tamed the wild unicorn.*

1938 the Cloisters has housed the medieval collection of the Metropolitan Museum of Art. Hundreds of thousands of visitors have strolled through the courtyards and passageways and looked at its paintings, illustrated manuscripts, and stained-glass windows. But the highlight of the collection is the Unicorn Tapestries, a set of tapestries also known as *The Hunt of the Unicorn.*

The Unicorn Tapestries

Created around 1500, probably in Brussels, Belgium, the set consists of 7 tapestries—heavy cloth wall hangings woven with designs and scenes—that measure 12 feet (3.7m) high and up to 14 feet (4.3m) wide. Owned by the same French family for generations, the tapestries were purchased by oil billionaire John D. Rockefeller Jr. in 1922 and donated to the Metropolitan Museum of Art in 1937. The unknown weavers of the Unicorn Tapestries used dyed wool and silk thread to create richly detailed pictures that told a story involving a hunting party of nobles, servants, and dogs who go on a hunt for a unicorn. They spot the unicorn, along with other animals, at a fountain. They attack; the unicorn fights them off and escapes, only to be eventually captured, slain, and taken to a castle. In the last panel, however, the unicorn is once again alive, but is being kept captive in a garden.

The unicorn in the tapestries itself appears as a beautiful yet powerfully mysterious white creature. The Unicorn Tapestries, which have proven immensely popular in the United States, have done much to cement a certain visual image of the unicorn in the minds of the American public. Writer and unicorn researcher Nancy Hathaway describes this image as "a graceful, horse-like animal, creamy white, with a long spiraling horn, cloven hoofs, a curled beard, and a delicately plumed tail."[2] To this day, many pictures of unicorns feature similar elements, and most people today think of unicorns as white horses sporting a single spiraling horn (though perhaps without the beard).

But unicorn literature and art abound with animals that bear little resemblance to this familiar image. Unicorn legends and stories can be found in many different cultures in many parts of the world, but the appearance, behavior, and magical properties of these creatures can vary starkly from place to place. In fact, many of the oldest surviving accounts and stories of the unicorn are among the most different. One of the mysteries surrounding the unicorn is how and whether these old stories somehow evolved into or are connected with the familiar creature featured in the Unicorn Tapestries that most people recognize today.

The Chinese Unicorn

Unicorns figure in the mythology of ancient China, for example, but they do not resemble the white horse of the Unicorn Tapestries. Chinese unicorns are described as having the head and body of a stag or deer, the tail of an ox, and the legs and hooves of a horse. In some accounts, they also possess the green scales of a dragon and a voice like a bell. Its single horn could grow to 12 feet (3.7m) long and was not hard like a spear but rather soft and fleshy. It was covered in fur in 5 colors considered special by the Chinese: red, yellow, blue, white, and black. Odell Shepard, a renowned British scholar of unicorn art, archaeology, and literature, notes that accounts of the Chinese unicorn are consistent regarding its appearance and almost always describe it as "gentle, beneficent, delicate in diet, regular and stately in pace."[3]

Called the ki-lin or qilin (pronounced "chee-lin")—a combination of *qi* (male) and *lin* (female)—the Chinese unicorn was one of four special animals who lived in the heavens (the other three being the dragon, the phoenix, and the tortoise). However, they would appear on earth on rare occasions to herald the birth of a wise person or benevolent emperor or otherwise to intervene in human affairs. Five thousand years ago, according to Chinese myth, a unicorn taught the emperor Fu Hsi the secrets of written language. In 551 B.C. a Chinese unicorn appeared before a young

pregnant woman, placed its head on her lap, and gave her a small jade stone. Carved on the stone was a poem predicting that she would bear a son who would become a ruler without a throne. Her son turned out to be Confucius, a revered and influential Chinese philosopher whose teachings and writings have shaped Chinese culture as much as any emperor has. For most of China's history, pictures of the ki-lin were displayed in the rooms of pregnant women in the hope of granting them the good luck of bearing distinguished sons.

Could this animal featured in Chinese mythology somehow be related to the unicorn that Westerners are familiar with—the one that appears in the Unicorn Tapestries? Some scholars believe so. Shepard believes that some connection may well exist. He writes:

> Distinct as the ki-lin seems at first to be from the Western unicorn, . . . it is hardly possible to think of him at last as an entirely independent creation. His different colouring, his more actively humane disposition, even the subtle but significant change in his horn . . . all these are due to his Chinese environment. On the other hand, he has the body of the stag and the solid hoof of a horse, . . . [and] like all Western unicorns, he is solitary, and he cannot be captured. It seems likely, therefore, that the ki-lin and the unicorn of the West have a common ancestor.[4]

The Japanese version of the unicorn, the kirin, was sometimes similar in appearance, but is also depicted as resembling a lion with one horn. Unlike its Chinese counterpart, the kirin's horn was a hard weapon capable of killing the wicked and protecting the virtuous. The kirin was said to be able to discern whether a person was good or wicked and thus was conveniently employed as both judge and executioner at criminal trials. Today the kirin is best known as the trademark symbol of Kirin beer; its image is found in numerous advertisements in Japan.

The Unicorn Boy of India

A very different unicorn is found in the ancient religious literature of India. In this case, the unicorn is not an animal but a boy or young man with a single horn growing from his head.

A version of the story comes from Book 3 of the *Mahabharata: The Book of the Forest*. Written around 200 B.C., the *Mahabharata* (which means "great story" in Sanskrit) with its collections of myths and ancient stories is one of the foundational documents of the Hindu religion. Book 3 tells the story of Kasyapa (or Vibhandaka—alternate spellings abound in the English translations), who left his family as a boy to become a holy man dedicated to mystical meditation. After the death of his teacher, Kasyapa shunned human company and lived in the forest with only animals for company. One day he encountered a beautiful doe deer or antelope; the animal ended up staying with him in his hut and, some months later, giving birth to a baby son. (There seem to be differing explanations of exactly how this happened; one account has Kasyapa spilling his "seed" in the lake water which the doe then drinks, but other stories state the doe became pregnant just by seeing the hermit's body.)

The child, named Risharinga or Rsyasrnga ("antelope horn") was a normal and handsome human boy except for one horn growing out of his forehead. The doe-mother soon died, and

Risharinga was raised by his father and away from other humans—a child of the forest who lived peacefully with its creatures. His horn served as a marker of his special, even divine, nature. Writer James Cross Giblin says:

> The gentle unicorn man provided a fine example of Hindu religious ideals in action. We may wonder how Risharinga's mother could be a doe antelope, but Hindu readers and listeners would have understood that she was a divine maiden who had been put under a curse by evil spirits. Such transformations happen frequently in Hindu literature, just as they do in European fairy tales. Hindus would also have recognized that Risharinga's horn symbolized the divine qualities of sensitivity and compassion that he had inherited from his mother.[5]

Although its appearance is quite different from what most of us envision a unicorn to be, many scholars believe that the unicorn boy of India may have influenced unicorn stories in other parts of the world. Matti Megged in his study of unicorn lore suggests, "It is quite possible that Indian myth, or some of its ingredients, wandered from India to Persia and from there to the Hellenistic [Greek] world, and was revived in Medieval and Renaissance art and poetry."[6]

The Persian Unicorn
Continuing west, from the Orient through India to Persia (now Iran), one finds a very different one-horned creature. Tales of this

unicorn form part of the beliefs of the Zoroastrian faith, an ancient Persian religion dating back to at least the seventh century B.C. According to the Zoroastrian religion, all parts of existence are part of a duality of good and evil. This includes animals, who are servants either of Ormuzd, god of light and good, or Ahriman, god of darkness and evil. Ahriman would send impure animals to contaminate water (one could well imagine water safety being an important problem in the Persian desert). But Ormuzd had his animal-servants as well. German scholar Rüdiger Robert Beer summarizes one version of the Zoroastrian myth:

> A three-legged ass, tall as a mountain, with six eyes and nine muzzles stands in the midst of the ocean. It has a golden horn with openings from which a hundred smaller horns sprout. . . . With the horn it crushes all hostility of ill-intentioned animals. When it lowers its head into the ocean, it causes a great commotion in the waters which then surge over the shores. When it calls out, all good female aquatic animals become pregnant and all the bad ones barren. When it urinates into the waters they become purified, and if it does not make water they all become tainted with the venom of Ahriman. In the dualist Zoroastrian religion, a one-horned ass stands beside Ormuzd and the powers of good.[7]

Some translations and accounts paint a picture of a 3-legged, one-horned creature as big as a mountain, with 9 huge mouths, with massive feet, and 6 eyes, including 2 on the top of its head and 2 on its hump. This seems even more far-removed from the unicorn in the tapestries than the ki-lin or the unicorn boy. Yet there is the interesting reference to purifying the water—a common theme in Western unicorn lore. In the second of the Unicorn Tapestries, the unicorn is dipping its horn in a pond, making its water pure and safe for it and other animals to drink.

Another animal found in tales from ancient Persia and Arabia was called the karg or karkadann. Like the Chinese ki-lin, this animal was rarely seen by humans. But the karkadann was not a godlike beast who only appeared before specially chosen people. Instead, it was simply a solitary wild animal that avoided humans. Unlike the gentle and civilized ki-lin, the karkadann was a fierce brute that could and would battle all animals, including elephants. In one Arabian story, a karkadann successfully gored and killed an elephant, only to have it stuck on its horn. Weakened by battle and unable to move under the weight of the elephant, the karkadann (along with the elephant) was taken by a roc—a huge bird of prey featured in Arabian myths—and fed to its chicks.

The karkadann was said to be as big as a rhinoceros and have three hooves in each foot and the tail of a lion. But visual descriptions of the beast vary widely; some describe it as a horse, while others have it resembling an ox or an actual rhinoceros. But the stories do consistently describe the karkadann as a fierce animal that other creatures tried to avoid—with the exception of a bird called the ringdove. The bird's songs were so soothing to the ferocious beast that it would lie peacefully and even allow the bird to perch on its horn.

According to legend, the karkadann could sometimes be successfully hunted, but never tamed—except by one man. That person was Alexander the Great (356–323 B.C.), a Macedonian prince who created an empire that stretched eastward from Egypt to the borderlands of India. His mount during his military campaigns was named Bucephalus, a horse in some accounts, a karkadann or unicorn (with tail feathers like a peacock) in others. The story goes that Alexander, age 13, volunteered to try to ride the animal after no one in his father's kingdom could be found to do so. By approaching the animal with gentleness and showing no fear, Alexander was able to tame and ride it. Bucephalus went on to become Alexander's devoted companion and a fierce warrior in his own right.

Greek and Roman Accounts

Alexander the Great's historical importance stems in part from his role as a bridge between Eastern and Western cultures. He was one of the earliest historical figures of the ancient Greek and Roman civilizations, which in turn are considered to be the foundations of Western civilization. Like the Persians, Indians, and Chinese, the ancient Greeks and Romans created a rich collection of stories about mythological beasts such as centaurs, gargoyles, and fauns. But the unicorn was never part of their religion or mythology. The ancient Greeks and Romans apparently considered the unicorn to be a real—if exotic—animal.

The earliest known description of unicorns in Western literature was written about 2,400 years ago, shortly before Alexander the Great's birth. The author, Ctesias (pronounced "*tee*-see-us") was a Greek physician. In 416 B.C. he accepted an appointment to work for the Persian emperor. After working in the emperor's court for 17 years, he returned to his Greek home around 398 B.C. and authored several volumes based on what he saw and heard

"When [the Persian unicorn] calls out, all good female aquatic animals become pregnant and all the bad ones barren."
— According to a Zoroastrian myth.

in Persia. Most of his writings have been lost, but surviving fragments include the following passage:

> There are in India certain wild asses which are as large as horses, and larger. Their bodies are white, their heads dark red, and their eyes dark blue. They have a horn on the forehead which is about a foot and a half in length. The dust filed from this horn is administered in a potion as a protection against deadly drugs. The base of this horn . . . is pure white; the upper part is sharp and of a vivid crimson; and the remainder, or middle portion, is black. . . . The animal is exceedingly swift and powerful, so that no creature, neither the horse nor any other, can overtake it.[8]

The India that Ctesias writes about is a general term meaning the mysterious lands east of the Persian Empire, including the Himalaya Mountains and Tibet. He is not describing a demigod or mythological creature, but an actual animal based on travelers' tales and other secondhand accounts. His descriptions of a unicorn influenced other Greek and Roman texts that sought to catalog and describe the world's animals. They reappeared in the writings of the famed Greek philosopher Aristotle (384–322 B.C.). Aristotle apparently distrusted the reliability of much of what the good doctor had reported (among other animals Ctesias described was the manticore—a man-eating beast with the face of a man, three rows of teeth, a lion's body, and a scorpion's tail), but Aristotle did accept the view that unicorns existed. He wrote: "There are . . . some animals that have one horn only,

Aristotle devised a theory that animals with solid hoofs were more likely to have no horns or only one horn than cloven-hoofed animals, arguing that since hoofs and horns were made of the same substance, solid-hoofed animals had less of the material left over for horns. Aristotle's brief discussion of unicorns was enough to establish them as real in the minds of educated people for centuries afterward.

for example, the oryx, whose hoof is cloven, and the Indian ass, whose hoof is solid. These creatures have their horn in the middle of their head."[9] Aristotle also devised a theory that animals with solid hoofs were more likely to have no horns or only one horn than cloven-hoofed animals, arguing that since hoofs and horns were made of the same substance, solid-hoofed animals had less of the material left over for horns. Aristotle's brief discussion of unicorns was enough to establish them as real in the minds of educated people for centuries afterward.

References to unicorns can also be found in ancient Roman sources. Julius Caesar (100–44 B.C.) was a famous general who led Roman armies into what is now England, Germany, and France. He sent reports back to Rome about his military campaigns, and in one, he mentioned an animal that lived in the Hercynian forest by the Rhine River. This forest, Caesar wrote, was so big that a person journeying for 60 days would not cross it. This is all the general wrote in the first-known report of unicorns in Europe:

> It is known that many kinds of wild beasts not seen in other places breed therein, of which the following are those that differ most from the rest of the animal world and appear worthy of record. There is an ox ["bos"] shaped like a stag, from the middle of whose forehead, between the ears, stands forth a single horn, taller and straighter than the horns we know.[10]

Pliny the Elder (A.D. 23–79), a Roman scholar, wrote an influential natural history of animals that included a brief description of the unicorn from India that compared it to a horse. The unicorn was "an exceedingly wild beast . . . which has a stag's head, elephant's feet, and a boar's tail, the rest of the body being like that of a horse. It makes a deep lowing noise, and one black horn two cubits long projects from the middle of its forehead. This animal, they say, cannot be taken alive."[11] A similar description is preserved in a fragment by Aelian, an Italian who lived in the second century A.D. at the height of the Roman Empire. His *De Animalium Natura* was a compilation of writings from earlier sources. It includes one of the first descriptions of a spiraled horn:

> They say there are mountains in the interior regions of India which are inaccessible to men and therefore full of wild beasts. Among these is the unicorn, which they call the "cartazon." This animal is as large as a full-grown horse, and it has a mane, tawny hair, feet like those of an elephant, and the tail of a goat. . . . Between its brows there stands a single black horn, not smooth but with certain natural rings, and tapering to a very sharp point. . . . With beasts of other species that approach it the "cartazon" is gentle, but it fights with those of its own kind. . . . It seeks out the most deserted places and wanders there alone. In the season of rut it grows gentle toward the chosen female and they pasture side by side, but when this time is over he becomes wild again and wanders alone.[12]

Overall, while people of ancient Greece and Rome appeared to have believed in animals with one horn, they did not make

Was the Chinese Unicorn Really a Giraffe?

Author and book editor Georgess McHargue writes in her book *The Beasts of Never* that the African giraffe might possibly be the inspiration for the Chinese unicorn, or ki-lin, also spelled *Ch'i-lin*:

> It is very interesting that in the fifteenth century, when Chinese sailors began to make their first regular voyages to the eastern coast of Africa, one of the greatest prizes to be brought back to the imperial court was a live giraffe—an animal that the Chinese immediately identified with

unicorns a central feature of their culture and mythology. There are no preserved Greek or Roman paintings or other artwork of unicorns. They did not develop a trade in unicorn horns. While giraffes (called "camelopards"), elephants, and other exotic

the Ch'i-lin. In fact, the giraffe does have some characteristics that resemble those of the Ch'i-lin surprisingly closely. Like the Ch'i-lin it is of a peaceable disposition and eats no flesh. Its back is spotted with several colors of brown and its belly is yellowish. Its tail is tufted like that of the ox and, most strikingly, its horns (though there are two and not one) end in knobs or tufts of hair, a highly unusual feature not found on any other animal. Perhaps strangest of all is the fact that in the Somali language, . . . the word for giraffe is *girin*, and Chinese scholars note that the spelling "ch'i-lin" is about as close as the Chinese language can come to pronouncing the Somali word.

Georgess McHargue, *The Beasts of Never.* New York: Delacorte, 1987, p. 75.

animals were regularly featured in Roman triumphal marches and circuses, there is no recorded instance of an actual *unicornis* being displayed. Furthermore, the few written descriptions of unicorns they produced still seem far away from the graceful white unicorn of the Unicorn Tapestries.

An early written description of unicorns that differs from other accounts comes from a book created sometime between A.D. 100 and 400. It was a collection of descriptions and stories about birds, animals, and fish, and each entry began by saying, "Physiologus (the naturalist) says—." The whole collection became known as the *Physiologus.* Scholars believe it was written in Alexandria, Egypt, but no original manuscript survives today. The following extract is taken from a Latin translation published in the ninth century: "Physiologus says that the unicorn has this nature. He is a small animal, like a kid, but exceedingly fierce, with one horn in the middle of his head; and no hunter is able to capture him."[13]

Margaret B. Freeman, former art curator of the Cloisters and author of a book on the Unicorn Tapestries, is among many who have noted that the *Physiologus* seems to describe an almost entirely dissimilar animal from the unicorns found in other Greek and Roman sources. Freeman writes: "The unicorn of the *Physiologus* is startlingly different from the magnificent animal of Ctesias, Pliny, and Aelian. He is no longer likened to a horse or an ass larger than a horse. He is . . . only a small goat, a kid." Shepard notes that the *Physiologus* and the books it inspired had a great influence over how the unicorn would be pictured. "Not Ctesias and not Aelian but this grist of old wives' tales fathered upon an imaginary 'Physiologus' was responsible for scattering the image of the unicorn throughout Europe, making him familiar where books were never read, . . . depicting him in stained glass and on tapestry."[14]

The unicorn of the Unicorn Tapestries seems to reflect a combination of ancient influences. Freeman writes: "The unicorn of the tapestries retains the horse-like appearance of the unicorn of Pliny. However, he has as well the beard and cloven hooves of the goat, following the description in the *Physiologus*. The visual result of this combination is satisfying, even superb."[15]

This artistic creation is arguably not only the work of the creators of the tapestries, but of the medieval culture from which they sprang. In examining how the unicorn was seen in medieval times, researchers have looked at two influential books of the Middle Ages: the *Physiologus* and the Holy Bible.

CHAPTER 2

The Unicorn in Medieval Times

The Unicorn Tapestries displayed at the Cloisters in New York City were created around 1500. This was at the end of the Middle Ages, a distinct period in European history that ran about 1,000 years from the fall of the Roman Empire in A.D. 476 to Christopher Columbus's voyages to the New World in 1492. This middle era between ancient and modern times was a period when many people believed in unicorns and produced an enormous outpouring of unicorn-related literature and art. Recurring themes and symbolic uses of the unicorn, many of which are found in the Unicorn Tapestries, appear time and again. This was not the case in ancient Greece or Rome, or in Europe prior to the Middle Ages; part of the mystery of the unicorn is how and why this animal became so prominent in medieval culture.

Roughly two or three centuries before Jesus was born, scriptures were translated from the original Hebrew into Greek. Many scholars now believe that it was this event that introduced unicorns into the Bible. In Christian writing the unicorn's single horn represented one God—and the unity that (according to Christian doctrine at that time) existed between God the father and Jesus the son. This is a woodcut of a unicorn and the pope.

Religion—specifically Christianity—plays a central part in answering this particular mystery. After the Roman Empire fell, its former realm and the rest of Europe were divided for most of the following millennium into a patchwork quilt of warring fiefdoms, small kingdoms, and tribal states. Trade and cultural interchange dried up; the vast majority of Europeans lived as peasant farmers bound to local lords and who seldom ventured away from their communities. However, there remained one vestige of the Roman Empire that provided a unifying cultural influence—the Christian Church. Headquartered in Rome, its influence spread steadily throughout Europe over the next few centuries as missionaries were sent to convert local rulers to the Christian faith. The church played a role in the political affairs of states and was a major patron of the arts. In an era when many people could not read, books and learning were preserved in monasteries and convents peopled by monks and nuns who had pledged themselves to Christian devotion. Many monasteries became significant landowners and a major force in government. Libraries were preserved and books themselves painstakingly copied by hand inside these religious orders.

To teach moral and religious lessons to people who could not read, church-sponsored art developed a complex system of iconography—images that symbolized different aspects and stories of the Christian faith. Most of the unicorn art and writing of this period depicts Christian themes and stories from the Bible and other religious books. This raises the question of how unicorns came to gain importance in Christian art and teaching. The answer to that mystery begins with the story of how unicorns came to be in the Bible in the first place.

Unicorns in the Bible

The Bible is a collection of writings from different authors at different times. Christians divide the Bible into 2 parts: the Old Testament and the New Testament. The Old Testament consists of the scriptures that describe the origins and history of the Jewish people and the religion of Judaism. Roughly 2 or 3 centuries before Jesus—the founder of Christianity and the subject and inspiration of the New Testament—was born, these scriptures were translated from the original Hebrew into Greek. Many scholars now believe that it was this event that introduced unicorns into the Bible.

The story goes like this: In 250 B.C., a time when the Jewish people had no nation of their own and were scattered around the Mediterranean area, 72 Jewish scholars in Alexandria, Egypt, were taken to an island by Ptolemy II of Egypt to translate their holy scriptures from Hebrew into Greek, the predominant language in the region. Their finished product became known as the Septuagint, meaning "seventy"—the number of days the scholars needed to complete their work (Whether or not events happened exactly this way, what is beyond dispute is the creation of a Greek translation of the Hebrew scriptures in the centuries immediately before Christ's birth).

One of the challenges these scholars faced arose from several references to an animal called the *re'em* (pronounced "ray-em") that had no obvious translation. The animal's appearance was not described in great detail, but it was presented as powerful, untamable, and awe inspiring. Today many modern scholars believe the *re'em* refers to an aurochs, a wild ox that was the ancestor of domestic cattle but had already gone extinct in the Middle

East. Scientists working from fossil remains estimate that the aurochs might have been as large as 12 feet (3.7m) long and 7 feet (2m) tall, with a large pair of horns. But the Alexandrian scholars, generations removed from their pastoral roots, and quite possibly aware of the writings of Aristotle and Ctesias, settled on the Greek word *monoceros* (one horn) as their translation of *re'em*.

Their decision had lasting repercussions. When the Septuagint was translated into Latin by Saint Jerome in the fourth century, the word became *unicornis* (although Jerome did use "rhinoceros" in some of the verses). The Vulgate, or Latin translation, was the standard Bible authorized by the Christian Church for most of the Middle Ages. Martin Luther kept unicorns in his influential German translation, as did the creators of the early English translations; the famous 1611 King James Version has seven references to unicorns. As writer Nancy Hathaway observes, "References in the Bible in large part account for the entrance of the unicorn into European consciousness. . . . And because the animal was mentioned in the Bible, its existence could certainly not be doubted; the word of God attested to it."[16] In other words, people in medieval times believed that unicorns were real, even though they had never seen them, simply because they appeared in the Bible.

Noah and the Unicorns

One of the places unicorns appear in artwork and stories is within another Biblical tale that was accepted as fact during the Middle Ages—the story of Noah's ark. According to the book of Genesis in the Old Testament, God was angry with the people he had created, and he caused a great flood to essentially start things over. But prior to the rainfall, God enlisted the one righteous person left—Noah—to build a great ark. This was not only to save Noah and his family, but to preserve a male and female of every type of animal from the flood. In the original Biblical account, Noah does successfully save all the world's animal species.

During the Middle Ages, various folktales and artistic depictions arose to explain why unicorns, despite Noah's efforts, were not rescued with the other animals. In some accounts, they arrived too late to board the ark. In others, they acted so haughtily over the other animals that an angered Noah booted them from the boat. In one Jewish folktale, the proud unicorn insisted he could swim and did not need any help. The unicorn proceeded to swim for 40 days and 40 nights until the rains stopped. Noah then released all the birds to look for land. The unicorn followed them as they searched in vain for a place to rest. Eventually the birds, too far away and too exhausted to return to the ark, all landed on the horn of the tired unicorn, and their combined weight ultimately drowned the noble beast.

None of these stories actually appear in Genesis. Unicorns are not mentioned at all in the Old Testament account of the flood. But these stories did provide people in medieval times an explanation to the mystery of why no one saw unicorns anymore, even though their existence was attested to in the Bible.

Christian Symbolism

References to unicorns in the Bible, in its Greek and Latin translations, conferred the authority of the word of God to the idea that unicorns were real. But many early Christian saints went further and argued that the unicorn could be seen as a symbol of Christianity's founder, Jesus Christ. The unicorn's single horn represented one God—and the unity that (according to

Christian doctrine) existed between God the Father and Jesus the Son. Saint Ambrose (340–397), bishop of Milan, expressed some doubts that unicorns actually existed but argued for their importance as religious symbols; "Who is this unicorn [mentioned in Psalms] but the only begotten Son of God?"[17] Saint Basil (330–379) wrote that Jesus "will be called the son of unicorns, for as we have learned in [the biblical book of] Job, the unicorn is irresistible in might and unsubjected to man. . . . Christ is the power of God, therefore he is called the unicorn on the ground that He has one horn, that is, one common power with the Father."[18] Making the unicorn a symbol of Jesus Christ inspired not only church sermons in this era, but many unicorn depictions in religious art, stained-glass windows, wood carvings, and book illustrations during the Middle Ages.

The *Physiologus* and Medieval Bestiaries

The unicorn's role as an icon of Christ is due not only to its mention in the Bible and in the writings of early church fathers, but also to the *Physiologus,* a collection of animal descriptions and legends that was comparable to the Bible in its influence and popularity. The *Physiologus* (the "naturalist" or "book of nature") was written sometime between A.D. 100 and 400, probably in Alexandria, Egypt; its exact origins are themselves a mystery. Over the next thousand years, it was translated into many languages, including Arabic, Latin, Armenian, German, Anglo-Saxon, and even Icelandic. Over time people added animals, real and imaginary, to enlarged versions known as bestiaries.

Within the *Physiologus* and other bestiaries were descriptions of common animals such as the fox and the hedgehog, exotic animals such as the lion, giraffe, and camel, and even more exotic ani-

People in medieval times believed that unicorns were real, even though they had never seen them, simply because they appeared in the Bible. Just as the unicorn mysteriously surrenders its power and independence to the maiden in this story, Jesus, according to Christian belief, surrendered his divine nature and powers and became a human by means of the Virgin Mary, his mother. This woodcut is from a story about a unicorn taking refuge with the Virgin Mary.

mals such as the dragon, the manticore, the griffin, and the phoe-nix. Each animal entry featured both physical descriptions and, just as important, moral and theological lessons. For example, the ant exemplified industry, the fox deviousness, and the hedgehog prudence. Many animals were also interpreted to be symbols of religious figures and stories. The result, writes medieval scholar John Williamson, was a "conglomeration of natural history, fables, legends, and mythology shaped to convey an understanding of the scriptures and conduct of a good Christian."[19]

Perhaps the story in the *Physiologus* that most captivated its medieval audience was its tale of how the unicorn could be caught. This excerpt is taken from a ninth-century version of the *Physiologus:* "No hunter is able to capture him. Yet he may be taken in this manner: men lead a virgin maiden to the place where he most resorts and they leave her in the forest alone. As soon as the unicorn sees her he springs into her lap and embraces her. Thus he is taken captive and exhibited in the palace of the king."[20]

The Maiden and the Unicorn

It is this particular story, and its introduction of the maiden, that has inspired more retellings, artwork, and other unicorn depictions than any other. From this time forward, writes author James Cross Giblin, "whether in medieval works of art or in modern stories about unicorns [a young girl] will almost always play a leading role."[21] The basic template of the story—the fierce and elusive unicorn is drawn to a pure young girl's lap and thus made vulnerable to capture—runs throughout the medieval unicorn literature. However, many of the accounts differ on various details. In early versions there are no hunters; the maiden herself leads the unicorn to the king's palace. Later versions and illustrations add hunters and hunting dogs. Sometimes the unicorn is captured alive; in other cases he is killed. In some cases the maiden grasps the unicorn by the horn or slips a bridle around its neck; in other stories the unicorn falls asleep in her lap. A few accounts suggest that dressing a man in women's clothes and perfumes could do the trick.

Where did this strange story about a maiden taming the unicorn come from? One theory is that this story has its origins in Indian myths about Risharinga, the unicorn boy of India. Risharinga, according to Indian legend, was the son of a Hindu hermit and a doe antelope or deer. He grew up with the animals in the forest and had a single horn growing from his head.

The story does not end there. It goes on to tell of a local kingdom that is being ravaged by drought. The king's advisors tell him that his past evil actions have angered the gods and that he must bring the unicorn boy back into human civilization. His horn, they say, has the power to appease the deities and bring rain. After some hesitation, the king dispatches his only child, a daughter, to the forest; Shanta is the first human besides his father that Risharinga has met. The innocent unicorn boy is enchanted by the girl, and she by him. He disregards his father's warnings about the dangers of female temptation and leaves the forest with her. He is taken to the king. He becomes angry when she tells him why she was sent to him, but when he sees how the drought has devastated the countryside, he weeps—and the rain falls.

Researchers have noticed numerous parallels between this story and the one in the *Physiologus*. In both cases the unicorn resides alone and free in the forest. In both cases it is a female that is sent to captivate and capture him. In both cases the unicorn is taken to the king's palace. "This is without doubt the source of the *Physiologus* narrative," argues unicorn researcher Rüdiger Robert Beer. "Somewhere along the line of its journey [from India to Egypt] this story became not one about a man called

Unicorn but one of the fabulous beast unicorn."[22] The Indian origins of this story may help explain why unicorns have often been portrayed in ways that accentuate certain human qualities, such as gallantry, innocence, and a vulnerability to feminine charms. "There are many similarities between the Indian myths and the European ones," argues Matti Megged in his study of unicorn lore, "the most striking of which is the human nature of the Unicorn, even though in European myth he is an animal, not human shaped."[23]

Symbolic Meanings

Most versions of the unicorn story in the *Physiologus* included commentary on its lessons for the believing Christian. Important to this teaching was how the unicorn symbolized aspects of the Christian story. Just as the unicorn mysteriously surrenders its power and independence to the maiden in this story, Jesus, according to Christian belief, surrendered his divine nature and powers and became a human by means of the Virgin Mary, his mother. Other commentaries have noted similarities with the Passion—the Christian story of the betrayal, execution, and resurrection of Jesus. The unicorn—considered fierce and impossible to capture, goes willingly to its death, much as Jesus, the powerful Son of God, willingly submitted to his execution. Finally, in some accounts, including the seventh tapestry of the Unicorn Tapestries, the unicorn reappears very much alive. This could symbolize the Christian belief that Jesus rose from the dead.

Such use of symbolic religious imagery reached its peak in the Middle Ages. The use of these images was viewed with suspicion by religious leaders and was part of the reason why some churches broke with the Roman Catholic Church in the Protestant Reformation of the 1500s. In 1563 the Roman Catholic Church officially decreed that depicting Jesus Christ as a unicorn—or any other animal or strange symbol—ran counter to church teachings. The church stopped commissioning or paying for unicorn art, and so such art's production greatly diminished.

A Symbol of Knighthood

Unicorns in medieval art were not always religious in theme. Unicorns also became closely associated with knights—the elite warriors of the Middle Ages—and their ideal of chivalry.

Chivalry is derived from the French word *chevalarie* which means "what the horse soldiers did." In the chaotic times following the fall of the Roman Empire, kings, dukes, and other local rulers sought to strengthen their hold on their feudal estates by hiring soldiers who could fight on horseback. The knights pledged their loyalty to the lord, or liege, who in turn would equip them with armor and weapons. In time these soldiers became known as knights, and they developed a reputation for upholding a strict code of ethics and behavior both on and off the field of battle.

To identify on the battlefield who was fighting for whom, knights were decorated with specific colors and designs on their cloaks, shields, armor, and helmets—a practice known as heraldry. Over time heraldic art was developed to identify noble families, fiefdoms, and entire nations. Animals were often used in coats of arms, and the unicorn was a popular choice to symbolize one's knightly identity. As unicorn scholar Odell Shepard writes, the unicorn

> was fierce and proud and dangerous to his foes, as a knight should be, and he was also strong; most significant of all, he was a protector and champion

Unicorn References in the Bible

The following references to unicorns in the Old Testament come from the 1611 King James Version of the Bible. Modern versions of the Bible generally use "wild ox" or a similar term in place of "unicorn."

"The voice of the Lord breaketh the cedars; yea, the Lord breaketh the cedars of Lebanon. He maketh them also to skip like a calf; Lebanon and Sirion like a young unicorn."

— Psalm 29:5–6

"But my horn shalt thou exalt like the horn of an unicorn: I shall be anointed with fresh oil."

— Psalm 92:10

"God brought them out of Egypt; he hath as it were the strength of a unicorn."

—Numbers 23:22

"Save me from the lion's mouth; for thou hast heard me from the horns of the unicorns."

— Psalm 22:21

"His glory is like the firstling of his bullock, and his horns are like the horns of unicorns: with them he shall push the people together to the ends of the earth."

— Deuteronomy 33:17

"And the unicorns shall come down with them, and the bullocks with their bulls; and their land shall be soaked with blood, and their dust made fat with fatness."

— Isaiah 34:7

"Will the unicorn be willing to serve thee, or abide by thy crib? Canst thou bind the unicorn with his band in the furrow? Or will he harrow the valleys after thee? Wilt thou trust him because his strength is great? Or wilt thou leave thy labour to him? Wilt thou believe him, that he will bring home thy seed, and gather it into thy barn?"

— Job 39:9–12

Robert III of Scotland in 1390, had two unicorns carved on the gateway to his castle. After his death in 1406, unicorns were incorporated in the Scottish royal arms and were embraced by the Scottish people as symbols of fierce devotion to one's country.

of other beasts against the wiles of their enemies. . . . Here was a perfect emblem of the ideal that European chivalry held before itself . . . the ideal according to which exceptional power and privilege were balanced and justified by exceptional responsibility.[24]

Shepard goes on to argue that the unicorn's popularity in heraldry may have itself inspired belief in the animal's existence in medieval times.

One can readily understand that during the Middle Ages, when coats of arms were not confined to stationary . . . but were pictures in vivid hues that went everywhere in the world—flaunting in state processions, resplendent at Court, rallying soldiers around their lords in battle—the frequent use of the unicorn upon heraldic crests would do much to increase the animals' vogue and to make it seem certain, if there had ever been any doubt, that he was as real as any beast of field or forest.[25]

The Lion and the Unicorn

One of the knights who adopted the unicorn as his symbol was Robert III, crowned king of Scotland in 1390. He had two unicorns carved on the gateway to his castle. He expressed the hope that they would bring him luck and help him be a stronger warrior and wiser ruler. After his death in 1406, unicorns were incorporated into the Scottish royal arms and were embraced by the

In 1603 England and Scotland were united under one king. By prior arrangement, James VI of Scotland was crowned king James I of England following the death of the childless Queen Elizabeth I. The new king created a new royal coat of arms that featured the lion and the unicorn. To this day the unicorn and the lion remain as official national symbols and bearers of the royal arms of Great Britain.

Scottish people as symbols of fierce devotion to one's country.

A well-known nursery rhyme probably refers to the conflict between Scotland and England, the latter of which had adopted the lion as its primary heraldic animal.

The Lion and the Unicorn
Fighting for the Crown
The Lion beat the Unicorn,
All about the Town.[26]

For centuries the English sought to conquer Scotland, while the Scots fought to maintain their independence. In 1603 the back-and-forth struggle came to an end when the two nations were united under one king. By prior arrangement, James VI of Scotland was crowned King James I of England following the death of the childless Queen Elizabeth I. The new king created a new royal coat of arms that featured the lion and the unicorn. To this day, centuries after knights have faded into history, the unicorn and the lion remain as official national symbols and bearers of the royal arms of Great Britain.

CHAPTER 3

Hunting the Unicorn

The oldest fragments of unicorn writing almost always refer to the difficulty of hunting or capturing the animal. Ctesias, the Greek physician who served in Persia, noted that the animal was faster than a horse or any other creature. The unicorn had other attributes besides mere speed, according to Cosmas Indicopleustes, a Greek merchant who traveled extensively around Ethiopia, the Red Sea, and the Persian Gulf. In A.D. 550 he wrote a book, *Christian Topography,* describing the places he had seen. The book includes this interesting story:

Although I have not seen the unicorn, I have seen four brazen pictures of him in the four-towered palace of the King of Ethiopia, and from these figures I have been able to draw a picture of him as you see. People say that he is a terrible beast and quite invincible, and that all his strength lies in his horn. When he finds himself pursued by many hunters and about to be taken he springs to the top of some precipice and throws himself over it, and in the descent he turns a somersault so that the horn sustains all the shock of the fall and he escapes unhurt.[27]

The picture Cosmas originally drew has been lost. Odell Shepard describes the picture in the ninth-century manuscript owned by the Vatican Library as showing "a beast of the antelope kind, apparently not large, very spirited in bearing, with a horn almost as tall as itself jutting perpendicularly from between its brows."[28]

Cosmas's story is typical of ancient unicorn literature that consistently describes the animal as difficult, if not impossible, to hunt or capture. In addition to the incredible bouncy horn, the unicorn has been described as solitary, wary of human contact, fleet of foot, and a strong and ferocious fighter when cornered. For people who believed in the actual existence of unicorns, these elusive qualities helped reconcile their belief with the fact that they had never seen one successfully hunted or captured.

The Unicorn Tapestries

Despite (or perhaps because of) its elusiveness, many of the unicorn tales that have captivated generations of storytellers have involved the successful hunt or capture of the animal. One of the most famous and elaborate depictions of the unicorn hunt is to be found in the Unicorn Tapestries on display in the Cloisters, part of the Metropolitan Museum of Art in New York City.

Created around 1500, the tapestries provide a detailed and realistic rendering of a hunting party of that period.

In the first tapestry, a group of hunters enter a forest. They are elaborately dressed; art scholars have used details of their clothes (including the shape of their shoes) to figure out when the tapestries were probably made. The hunter with a horn strapped around his shoulder seems to be the leader; he could well be the nobleman in whose realm the hunt takes place. The hunters are accompanied by hunting dogs and their keepers. The tapestries show the two types of dogs that were used in medieval hunts. There were the floppy-eared hounds who would track animals by scent and the slim and pointy-eared greyhounds who would run after the hunted animals after they had been spotted. In the upper right-hand corner of the tapestry, a scout in the woods raises a hand, signaling that a unicorn has in fact been sighted.

In the second tapestry, the hunters and their dogs are surrounding the unicorn and a host of other animals who are gathered next to a fountain. But the hunters do not immediately go after the unicorn. "According to the rules of the stag hunt," writes author James Cross Giblin, "they must wait until their quarry starts to run before they give chase."[29] The horn sounds and the chase begins in the third tapestry. The unicorn runs in a river, presumably to throw the hounds off his scent, but is not successful. In the fourth tapestry the surrounded unicorn fends off the hunters and their spears and attack dogs, responding with his horn and hooves. If he were an ordinary deer or stag, this would undoubtedly be the end of the hunt. But the unicorn lives up to his reputation. Although wounded, he successfully fights off the hunters and escapes to a garden in the next tapestry.

In this fifth tapestry (which unfortunately survives only in fragments) the unicorn is finally captured with the help of a maiden—a recurring theme in medieval literature and art about unicorns. An interesting version of this unicorn hunting story comes from Hildegarde von Bingen (1098–1179), a German nun and religious mystic who rose to become the abbess (chief administrator) of a large convent. In her account of unicorn hunting, instead of a single maiden lulling the unicorn to sleep on her lap, a group of young girls are, perhaps unwittingly, used as bait. Von Bingen writes:

> On the day of the hunt, men, women, and young girls pursue the unicorn. Then the girls separate from the others and go off to gather flowers in the meadow. The unicorn, upon seeing the girls, stops at once, crouches on his hind legs in the tall grass, and watches them for a long time. He falls in love with the girls, for he sees that they are gentle and kind. But while he is gazing at them, the hunters steal up behind and slay the unicorn and cut off his horn.[30]

The fifth tapestry is titled "The Unicorn Is Tamed by the Maiden." Unfortunately, that tapestry only survives in two partial fragments; all that can be seen of the maiden is a graceful hand gently stroking the unicorn's mane, while her friend signals the hiding hunters to strike.

In the sixth tapestry the maidens are gone, and the hunters in one corner are successfully slaying the unicorn with their spears. The rest of that tapestry shows the triumphal return of the hunters to the castle with the dead unicorn and its horn, which has been cut off, as the lord, lady, and friends await them.

Unicorns and Trees

In stark contrast to the large group of rich hunters, spotters, and dogs one finds in the Unicorn Tapestries, another famous tale of unicorn capture features a humble tailor acting alone. One of the German folktales collected by the Brothers Grimm in the 1800s, "The Brave Little Tailor," tells the adventures of a poor tailor who has to use his wits to fight giants and perform other tasks in order to win the princess's hand in marriage.

> "Before you can have my daughter and half the kingdom," [the king told the tailor] . . . "you will have to perform one more heroic deed. There's a unicorn out in the forest, and it's doing a lot of damage. I want you to capture it."
>
> "If two giants don't scare me off, why would I worry about a unicorn! . . ."
>
> The tailor went out into the woods with a rope and an ax. Once again he told the men who had been assigned to him to wait at the edge of the forest. He didn't have to wait long, for the unicorn appeared before long and rushed at the tailor, as if he were planning to just go ahead and gore him with his horn.
>
> "Easy, easy," he said. "Things don't happen that fast." And the tailor stood still and waited until the animal got up close, then he jumped nimbly behind a tree. The unicorn charged the tree with all its might and rammed his horn into it so hard that he couldn't get it back out again. And so it was caught. "Now I've got my little birdie," the

This computer-generated illustration shows a unicorn in the forest. Unicorns are said to be solitary creatures.

tailor said, and he came out from behind the tree and put a rope around the unicorn's neck. Then he took his ax and chopped the horn free of the tree. Once everything was all set, he led the animal off and took it to the king.[31]

The Hunter and the Unicorn:
A Tibetan Folktale

A very different twist on the unicorn hunt comes from this Tibetan folktale. It was one of several tales collected and translated by a missionary doctor and first published in English in 1925.

> ONCE, long ago when men's hearts were evil and they forgot to be grateful for kindness, a hunter was walking along the road and fell over a cliff, almost killing himself. As he was wondering how he could get to the road again, a unicorn came along, stopped and looked over at him. The man began to beg and plead, saying, "You are such a nice unicorn. I have never harmed any animal, except

This is a familiar story in unicorn lore that, like the method of taming unicorns with a maiden, reappears in various forms and tellings. One comes from a 1607 animal encyclopedia that includ-

when I was hunting and hungry, and I never would hurt you." He begged and coaxed until the unicorn came down and helped him up on the road again. When he was safely out he said, "Now I know the road out of here, so I have no more use for you." He grabbed his gun and shot the unicorn dead. Sure enough, it was a bad road and he wandered around and around, but could find no end, no way out, and wished he had asked the unicorn the right road before he had killed him. Finally growing tired and weak and hungry, and no one coming to help him, he fell down the cliff again and died.

Moral: Don't be sure you know more than you do.

A.L. Shelton, trans., *Tibetan Folk Tales.* St. Louis: United Christian Missionary Society, 1925.

ed information on elephants, camels, and dolphins in addition to beasts now believed to be mythological. The author, clergyman Edward Topsell (1572–1625), describes capturing a unicorn by trapping its horn in a tree, but with one important difference: the unicorn hunter happens to be a lion.

> As soone as ever a Lyon seeth a Unicorne, he runneth to a tree for succor, that so when the Unicorne maketh force at him, hee may not onely avoide his horne, but also destroy him; for the Unicorne in the swiftnesse of his course runneth against the tree wherein his sharpe horne sticketh fast, then when the Lyon seeth the Unicorne fastned by the horne without all danger, he fauleth upon him and killeth him. These things are reported by the king of *Aethiopia* in a Hæbrew Epistle unto the Bishop of *Rome*.[32]

The king of Ethiopia that Topsell mentions is very likely the famous, if mythical, Prester John. In the twelfth century, a letter addressed to the Pope (the Bishop of Rome) was purportedly sent by Prester John, a Christian king of a rich and powerful nation in Asia. Scholars now believe it was a creative composition by an unknown monk, but at the time many European leaders, including those who had been trying and failing to wrest Jerusalem from Muslim rule in the Crusades, were heartened by the idea of a previously unknown Christian kingdom existing in a hostile world. For the next 500 years or so, Prester John's letter would be recopied by hand, translated into different languages, and circulated throughout Europe. Over the course of all this transcribing and translating, the location of Prester John's kingdom somehow moved from Asia to Abyssinia (Ethiopia), the collection of its beasts grew more wondrous, and Prester John himself always seemed on the brink of some trouble or succumbing to heresy, even though he had apparently managed to live for hundreds of years. But most versions featured this particular unicorn-hunting story:

> There are in our land also unicorns who have in front a single horn of which there are three kinds: green, black, and white. Sometimes they kill lions. But a lion kills them in a very subtle way. When a unicorn is tired it lies down by a tree. The lion goes then behind it and when the unicorn wants to strike him with his horn, it dashes into the tree with such a force that it cannot free itself. Then the lion kills it.[33]

The Sun and the Moon

Some scholars have traced this story of the lion, unicorn, and entrapping tree back to ancient myths relating to astronomy and astrology—the study of the movement of the stars and planets in the sky. The unicorn in particular has long been associated with the moon and the lunar cycle. Many artistic representations of unicorns, one example of which is on a seat in a church in Stratford-upon-Avon, England, include a crescent moon over its head. "The animal is most readily associated with the new or crescent moon," writes Shepard, "which might indeed seem to dwellers by the sea to be leading the stars down to the water and to dip its own horn therein before they descend."[34]

Numerous archaeological artifacts from what is now Iraq and surrounding regions, some several thousands of years old, include pictures not only of a one-horned animal associated with the moon, but what looks like a lion and a unicorn in combat. A carving on a cosemetics box from ancient Ur (the Mesopotamian

The unicorn has long been associated with the moon and the lunar cycle. Seen here are the Monoceros and Canis Minor constellations.

birthplace of the Jewish patriarch Abraham) shows a lion gripping a one-horned beast with his teeth and claws. Other artifacts, including gem carvings, pottery remains, statues, carvings on walls, and images on cylinder seals, show similar images. Most scholars agree that these are symbolic representations of some kind. Many argue that the lion (and its mane) symbolizes the sun, and the unicorn (and its horn) is emblematic of the crescent moon. The tree represents the world or the underworld. Writer Georgess McHargue suggests that people long ago created a story to match what they observed in the night skies—the moon seeming to chase the setting sun across the sky, only to disappear below the horizon and vanish when the sun rises and daylight comes.

The complete story relates how the Unicorn chases the lion across the sky until the lion dodges behind the tree that grows at the root of the world. Then the Unicorn, charging straight ahead, pierces the tree with its horn and is held fast so that the lion can come out and devour it. But nothing is permanent in the cycles of astronomy; the new moon always follows the old. And so, in the legend, the Unicorn always returns with renewed life to chase the sun-lion again across the sky.[35]

Long after the astronomical meanings were forgotten, these ancient stories may well have been passed down through generations, and thus might have ultimately led to the Grimm fairy tale with the tailor capturing the charging unicorn in a tree.

Tips for Unicorn Trackers

Not all stories of unicorn hunting are to be found in old manuscripts, ancient myths, or folktales. One interesting story comes from a surprisingly recent source. Robert Vavra is like many modern-day hunters who seek out wild animals with cameras, not guns. Their hunting prizes are pictures hanging on their wall, not stuffed and mounted heads. Vavra is an acclaimed photographer whose books featuring horses, exotic travel scenes, and wildlife have sold more than 3 million copies.

One of his most famous books is *Unicorns I Have Known*. Published in 1983, the volume features striking photographs of what appear to be unicorns in various habitats—desert sand dunes, flowered meadows, snowy woods, and rustic red canyons. The unicorns in his book look like handsome horses, except for the spiraled horn growing from their foreheads and the occasional flower decorations on their manes. In the accompanying text, Vavra writes that his photographs faithfully captured face-to-face unicorn encounters, beginning with one in a jungle near Tamazunchale, Mexico, in 1968. Vavra writes of seeing a bluish light, then a mysterious eye, while photographing fireflies in the twilight:

> Slowly I lowered the camera from my face until I was staring at the patch of jungle before me. There was the eye. Above it, concealed here and there by the screen of leaves, was a slim object, over a foot in length, sparkling green in the darkness like a jeweled wand. I squinted, but it was too far away to be distinguishable. Again I slowly raised the camera, hoping that its short telephoto lens would magnify the object and reveal its identity. The eye was still there. So was the brilliant object above it. With all my concentration, I tried to steady the camera, took another deep breath, and again pressed my elbows to my sides. There were beetles, dozens of them, emerald green, moving slowly along the . . . the . . . the horn.
>
> The horn!
>
> It *was* a horn above the blue eye. It was! At last! It was a unicorn!
>
> Then my only thought became, *I must get a picture of it. If not, I'll be like the rest and no one will ever believe me.*[36]

Unfortunately, between Vavra's excitement and the unicorn's sudden flight, the picture turned out to be a blur. But over the next 15 years, Vavra writes in his book, he developed a close enough rapport with unicorns (much as his friend primate researcher Jane Goodall developed a familiarity with the chimpanzees she studied) to approach and photograph them. His success is all the more remarkable given what he describes as their striking ability to detect humans and vanish from sight.

Vavra's book even includes helpful, if somewhat rigorous, tips on how to spot unicorns on one's own. According to him, would-be unicorn hunters should not wear leather or anything made from dead animals, or pack food made from dead animals. They should forgo any use of perfume, toothpaste, mosquito lotion, or any other artificially scented substance, and should not carry any gun or other weapon, nor ropes or nets. They must not bring along dogs or horses (children are okay), and if they see a unicorn, they should not call for it or try to feed it. Wearing camouflaged clothing is of no help, according to Vavra, because "what determines acceptance by unicorns is a matter of the heart, not of the clothing. The key to successful observation is believing."[37]

The book was published in 1983, before the advent of photo editing software and digital photography. Since its publication, Vavra has continually received letters from readers asking if his photographs are of authentic unicorns, or instead are simply photographs of horses with the horns added in by special effects. He responds to these letters the same way he responded to the question in a 2003 profile. "All I can say is, when I look through a camera and see a white horse with a horn, I assume it could only be a unicorn."[38]

CHAPTER 4

The Unicorn's Magic Horn

The second panel of the Unicorn Tapestries shows the hunters spotting the unicorn. The white animal is at the bottom of the picture dipping his horn into a pond of water. This act is something found in many other paintings and written accounts. By dipping its horn, the unicorn was making the water safe for drinking for itself and other animals. (This is one reason unicorns were said to be difficult to find; the grateful animals would warn the unicorn of approaching hunters).

A classic description of this phenomenon comes from John of Hesse, a traveler who visited religious sites in the Holy Land in 1389:

> Near the field of Helyon there is a river called Mirah, the water of which is very bitter, into which Moses struck his staff and made the water sweet so that the Children of Israel might drink. And even

in our times, it is said, venomous animals poison
that water after the setting of the sun, so that the
good animals cannot drink of it; but in the morning, after the sunrise, comes the unicorn and dips
his horn into the stream, driving the poison from
it so that the good animals can drink there during
the day. This I have seen myself.[39]

This story is one example of a central part of unicorn lore—the
ability of the unicorn's horn to fight off poison and cure sickness.
Unicorn scholar Odell Shepard, who coined the word *alicorn* for

*Konrad
von Gesner, the
Swiss natural-
ist who wrote
a sixteenth-
century ency-
clopedia of
animals,
included this
woodcut in his
encyclopedia.*

the unicorn's horn, argues that belief in these medicinal properties was "the most interesting, the strangest, and the central belief about the unicorn."[40] The power of the horn was believed to exist separately from the unicorn itself; humans could remove the horn from the unicorn and use it for their benefit. Belief in this peaked during the late Middle Ages and the Renaissance when a thriving trade developed in the sale of alicorns and alicorn powder. Such unicorn horns did in fact exist and can be seen to this day in places like the Tower of London and Saint Mark's Cathedral in Venice. The horns seemed proof positive that unicorns themselves were indeed real, even if no one had ever actually seen them. As Konrad von Gesner, the Swiss naturalist who wrote a sixteenth-century encyclopedia of animals, states, the unicorn "must be on earth, or else its horn would not exist."[41]

Unicorn Horns in Ancient Literature

The unicorn horn has been an important part of the animal's lore since ancient times. Ctsesias, the Greek doctor credited with the first written account of mysterious Indian "wild asses" with one horn, made special note of the horn's properties:

> The dust filed from this horn is administered in a potion as a protection against deadly drugs. . . . Those who drink out of these horns, made into drinking vessels, are not subject, they say, to convulsions or to the holy disease [leprosy]. Indeed, they are immune even to poisons if, either before or after swallowing such, they drink wine, water, or anything else in these beakers.[42]

The beakers Ctesias described may have been made from rhino horn—which, like alicorns, has long been coveted for its supposed medicinal value. Writer James Cross Giblin notes that ancient peoples throughout the world have believed that the power of horned animals was concentrated in the horns they used for defense and attack. "So when that strength was concentrated in one great horn [instead of two], as in the Indian rhino and the unicorn, it's easy to understand why people thought the horn was doubly powerful."[43] Giblin also observes that the ruling priest-kings in ancient societies, including those of Persia and Assyria, often wore tall, pointed headdresses—perhaps as a symbolic statement of their own power and authority.

Ctesias's account survived by being cited and repeated in other ancient Greek and Roman sources. In addition to being an antidote, unicorn horns were also believed to have the power to act as an early-warning system. Cups, goblets, knives, and forks made from alicorn were supposed to sweat or show drops of water in the presence of poisoned food.

Why Poisoning Was Feared

The fear of death by poison was no small matter for a king or member of the nobility during the late Middle Ages. Unlike present-day doctors, physicians of the time did not have the ability to detect poison in the body nor the knowledge of how poisons worked. Thus, poisoning seemed an ideal way to get rid of political or personal enemies without being detected; the victim would simply appear to die from a mysterious illness. Another advantage of poison was that it could be rubbed on the victim's clothing, enabling the poison to penetrate the wearer's skin slowly. The fourteenth-century king John of Castile reportedly died from boats soaked with poison, while King Henry VI of England (1421–1471) may have been the victim of poisoned gloves.

Beginning in the late 1300s, an epidemic of mysterious deaths hit Europe, particularly Italy. As Shepard observes, "Urged on by the peculiar needs created by their political institutions, the Italians of the Renaissance carried this art and profession [of poisoning people] to wonderful heights."[44] Perhaps he had in mind Aqua Toffana, a woman who was said to have killed more than 600 people with tasteless and odorless "medicine," artfully packaged in bottles with saints painted on them. During the 1400s and 1500s, Shepard writes,

> scores of Italian scholars and physicians, most of them in the pay of great lords, pitted their learning and wits against the secret skill of the poisoner. The pharmacopæia was ransacked, ancient texts were searched, superstitions older than civilization were revived—but nothing would serve; the dukes and counts and captains and cardinals of Italy continued to die suddenly, mysteriously, and ... prematurely.[45]

This desperate search for a poison preventative and cure created a demand. Fortunately, a new product had become available to meet it.

Frederick III made a throne in 1665 with arms, legs, and supporting pieces believed to be made from unicorn horns.

The Alicorn Trade

Beginning around the year A.D. 1100, a new kind of horn began to appear in Europe. The horns were 6 to 8 feet (1.8m to 2.4m) or so in length. Unlike elephant tusks, they were straight, not curved. Unlike antelope horns, they had a distinctive spiral design, like two horns twisted around each other into one straight one. It seemed fairly obvious to all who saw them that they were unicorn horns.

They were also very rare, and they became a proud if costly possession of princes, emperors, nobility, and popes. An inventory of the royal wares of Queen Elizabeth I of England, made in 1558, the first year of her reign, included a unicorn horn with a recorded value of 10,000 pounds. This was enough money to buy a castle and country estate in those days. The 1468 marriage of Princess Margaret of York to Duke Charles the Bold of Burgundy featured "great unicorns' horns, very large and very beautiful"[46] according to one observer. Holy Roman emperor Charles V, who reigned in the sixteenth century, had a debt equal to roughly 1 million dollars in today's money that he paid off with 2 unicorn horns. Frederick III, the king of Denmark, made a throne in 1665 with arms, legs, and supporting pieces made from these horns.

One interesting story involves a unicorn horn still at New College, Oxford University, and Robert Dudley, the Earl of Leicester and a close friend of Queen Elizabeth I. His friendship with the queen raised suspicions that he wanted to marry her. These suspicions grew after his first wife died suddenly and foul play with poison was suspected. Dudley began to fear that his enemies at court might try to poison him. In 1576 he demanded help from officials at New College, Oxford, asking them to lend him their valuable alicorn. After some debate, a compromise was reached;

the officials sawed off the tip of the horn and sent it to Leicester. Dudley survived whatever plot he was worried about, but apparently never returned what they lent him. The horn remains at Oxford, minus its tip.

For others below noble rank who could not afford a whole unicorn horn, a trade developed in alicorn powder, scrapings, and bits of horn incorporated into cups or other utensils. A seventeenth-century advertisement by a physician listed numerous ailments that alicorn medicine could cure, including scurvy, ulcers, gout, coughs, heart palpitations, and even "Melancholly or Sadness."[47] Other diseases it was said to be able to cure included the plague and epilepsy. Small wonder that when the

Holy Roman emperor Charles V, who reigned in the sixteenth century, had a debt equal to roughly $1 million in today's money that he paid off with two unicorn horns.

Apothecaries Society of London was founded in 1617, it adopted a pair of unicorns as its symbolic coat of arms. From 1651 to 1741, every registered pharmacist in that city was required to have alicorn medicine in stock.

The Narwhal and the Inuit

For hundreds if not thousands of years the Inuit people of the Arctic have hunted the *kilaluga,* or narwhal. The Inuit relied on the whale's meat, blubber, and *muktuk* (its vitamin-rich, nutty-tasting skin) for sustenance for themselves and their sled dogs. Oil made from narwhal blubber lighted their stone oil lamps, while sinew taken from the narwhal's back was used as a strong leather-working thread for clothing, boots, and tents. In an environment with hardly any trees, the Inuit used the "horn" of the *tugalik* (the tusked, male narwhal) as lances, sled runners, and tent poles.

Testing for Counterfeits

The high prices that these medicines fetched naturally led to the selling of "fake" alicorn. Counterfeit alicorn powder was easy enough to make; one could use crushed bones from farm animals or fossils, or use limestone and clay. Fraudulent horns were harder to manufacture but were often fashioned or carved from elephant or walrus tusks that had been boiled, softened, and straightened.

Nobles and apothecaries thus needed a way to tell fake alicorn from the real thing. One effective experiment was reportedly used by King James I of England (1566–1625) after he paid more than 10,000 pounds for a unicorn horn. The king summoned a servant to drink some poison mixed with alicorn powder. Unfortunately for the king, he had apparently been cheated. Unfortunately for the servant, the experiment proved fatal.

Since using humans as guinea pigs was an option presumably only available to kings, other tests were more often used during this time. One accepted test was to place beakers carved from alicorn over a scorpion; if the scorpion died, the alicorn was genuine. Or one could draw a ring on the floor with the alicorn and place a spider within the circle; if the alicorn was genuine, the spider would not be able to cross the line and would starve to death. Another test was to place a horn in water to see if the water would begin bubbling. Other testers would lay the horn on top of a piece of silk placed on a burning coal, thinking that a true alicorn would prevent the silk from bursting into flame.

What the tests did not tell anyone was whether the alicorn, fake or real, really came from a unicorn at all. In the 1500s and 1600s, word slowly spread that what people thought was a unicorn horn worth 10 times its weight in gold was, in fact, the tooth of a mysterious whale—and probably not worth as much.

The Sea Unicorn

In 1577 a British sea captain named Martin Frobisher returned to London after exploring the Arctic in search of a northern sea route to Asia. He had failed in that quest but was able to present

Queen Elizabeth I with a special gift: the horn of a sea unicorn.

In July 1577 Frobisher's three ships had been hit by a severe storm. They sought refuge in a small harbor in Baffin Island, a large island at the extreme northeast corner of what is now Canada. There he and his crew found the floating body of "a great dead fish" along the shore. Frobisher wrote in his log that the animal was "round like a porpoise, being about twelve feet long," and had "a horn of two yards long growing out of the snout or nostrils."[48] Back then it was a commonly held belief that God created marine counterparts to all land animals. For example, there were land cows and sea cows, land horses and sea horses (walruses), and land bears and sea bears (fur seals), not to mention land serpents and sea serpents. So the first thought Frobisher and his crew had about their discovery was that they might have found a sea unicorn. They took its horn, which was broken at its tip, and tested it by putting poisonous spiders inside it. When it was reported the spiders had indeed perished, an excited Frobisher wrote in his log, "This horn . . . may truly be thought to be the sea-unicorn."[49] What he had actually found was not the counterpart to the mythical unicorn, but a mysterious whale called the narwhal.

A Trade Secret

The earliest known written description of this whale comes from *The King's Mirror,* a collection of Norse sagas dating back to the thirteenth century. In one section, a father tells his son of "the wonders that are found in the Icelandic seas."

> There is a sort [of whale] called the narwhal, which may not be eaten for fear of disease, for men fall ill and die when they eat it. This whale is not

large in size; it never grows larger than twenty ells [approximately 30 feet or 9m]. It is not at all savage but rather tries to avoid fisherman. It has teeth in its head, all small but one which projects from the front of the upper jaw. This tooth is handsome, well formed, and straight as an onion stem. It may grow to a length of seven ells [approximately 10 feet or 3m] and is as even and smooth as if shaped with a tool. It projects straight through forward from the head when the whale is traveling; but sharp and straight though it is, it is of no service as a defensive weapon; for the whale is so fond and careful of its tusk that it allows nothing to come near it.[50]

"There ain't no such animal!"

— A man exclaimed upon seeing a narwhal.

Narwhal flesh is not actually poisonous. This belief stems from its name which means "corpse whale" in Old Norse. The ancient Norse sailors might have thought the mottled, splotched coloring of the whale resembled the blotched gray hue of drowned sailors floating in the sea. Aside from that one error, the thirteenth-century description holds up well, especially in comparison with the more fanciful stories one finds in later accounts and whalers' tales, which described how narwhals ate corpses, used their tusks to spear 55-ton bowhead whales (50 metric tons), and even attacked and sank ships.

As the above account demonstrates, the Vikings who procured tusks from the native Inuit people were familiar with the narwhal centuries before Frobisher's voyage. But they were not too keen on publicizing where their valuable unicorn horns really came from. Trade records were kept obscure. While Norse

The tusk of the narwhal was sold as unicorn horn for hundreds of years. The Viking efforts at hiding the narwhal-unicorn connection were successful for five centuries.

Unicorns

settlers eagerly recorded the heroic deeds of the explorers and settlers in Greenland and Iceland, no sagas were made of voyages to the mysterious northern regions of Greenland, where it is believed most of the trade for narwhal tusk was made.

The Viking efforts at hiding the narwhal-unicorn connection were successful for five centuries. The fact that narwhals seldom ventured south of Greenland certainly helped preserve this trade secret. Another factor might be that the narwhal seems just as odd and unreal as any unicorn. "To a vast majority of people," marine biologist and author Fred Bruemmer writes, "the existence of a horselike animal carrying a wonder-working horn, vouched for by Aristotle, Pliny, and the Bible, seemed infinitely more believable than the existence of a whale with a ten-foot-long ivory tusk."[51]

Even when witnessed firsthand, it seems, the narwhal remains hard to believe in. Bruemmer tells the story of a mechanic who arrived in an Arctic settlement in the early 1960s and saw a narwhal being hauled ashore. "He walked over, looked at the tusked whale in wonder, and finally said, 'There ain't no such animal!'"[52]

The Secret Comes Out

Frobisher's gift was duly accepted as a genuine horn of a sea unicorn by Queen Elizabeth I and added to her collection. It is known today as the Horn of Windsor. However, Frobisher's discovery did lead some people to question whether the alicorns being sold in Europe actually came from unicorns. More and more references to the narwhal made their way into print. Gerhardus Mercator, in an atlas published in 1621, wrote, "Among the fish of Iceland is included the narwhal. It has a tooth in its head which projects to a length of as much as ten feet. Some sell this tooth as unicorn horn."[53] The grand duke of Moscow declined to purchase a beautiful alicorn after his private doctor told him it was the tooth of a fish.

Facing a weakening market, the merchants of Copenhagen, Denmark, enlisted a distinguished professor and physician named Ole Wurm to conduct an investigation of the true nature and origins of the alicorn. If they were hoping that he would prove the horns to be genuine and restore trust in their product, they chose the wrong person. Wurm not only proved to be honest and incorruptible but meticulous about his investigation. He got firsthand information about the narwhal from a bishop in Iceland who happened to be a former pupil. He collected numerous objects from all over the world, including the skull and horn supposedly taken from a unicorn, and examined them carefully. His conclusion, delivered in a public dissertation in 1638, was that alicorns were not horns at all, but have all the characteristics of teeth. The skull in his possession was a narwhal skull, and Wurm demonstrated how the narwhal tooth came out of the left side of the upper jaw.

Wurm's work can be seen as part of a new era in which direct observation and experimentation replaced reliance on old texts and authorities as a path to knowledge. When Wurm relayed his conclusions to Isaac de la Peyré, the French author wrote of having "great disputes with him because it overturns the opinions of all the old naturalists who have treated of unicorns . . . and it clashes with several passages of Holy Scripture, which can only be understood as having reference to unicorns with four feet."[54] Wurm was not persuaded to change his own observations or conclusions.

Wurm's dissertation did not mark the end of the unicorn trade by itself, but it was an important step in stripping the alicorn of some of its special aura. In Frankfurt, Germany, an ounce of alicorn pieces that cost 128 florins (gold pieces) in 1612 could be bought for only 8 florins in 1669. Unicorn horns began to be sold as walking sticks or decorations instead of miracle cures. John Quincy, compiling a 1749 edition of a reference book for pharmacists on medicines, wrote of the unicorn: "There are various opinions concerning this creature; . . . some strenuously contend that this horn is the tooth of a fish. The strange conceits of the medicinal virtues of this drug, are too numerous and too ridiculous to mention here; and both this and the following are now justly expelled [from] the present practice."[55] Thus alicorn joined other ancient remedies to be discarded by modern science.

CHAPTER 5

What Animals Inspired the Unicorn Stories?

If the unicorn horn everyone recognized was in fact the tooth of a whale, as more and more people came to believe after Martin Frobisher's 1577 encounter with the narwhal, where did that leave the unicorn? The discovery that unicorn horns were not actually unicorn horns did seem to cast doubt on the unicorn's very existence. For those who persisted in believing in the unicorn, a new hope lay in the epic discoveries being made in the New World and elsewhere.

The voyages of Columbus touched off a new era in which Europeans explored, settled, and colonized lands in North America, South America, Africa, Australia, and Asia. It was a time when new species were being discovered along with new lands. By the beginning of the eighteenth century, science writer Richard Conniff notes, "Every ship coming home from Africa, Asia, and the Americas seemed to carry some bizarre new creation: an opossum appeared on the crowded London quays, an iguana in

Antwerp, a chambered nautilus shell in Paris."[56] Could a unicorn be next?

North America provided precious few unicorn sightings. Olfert Dapper, a doctor in New Amsterdam (now New York), for example, wrote of one in his 1673 book *Die Unbekante Neue Welt:*

> On the Canadian border, there are sometimes seen animals resembling horses, but with cloven hoofs, rough manes, a long straight horn upon the forehead, a curled tail like that of the wild boar, black eyes, and a neck like that of a stag. They live in the loneliest wildernesses and are so shy that the males do not even pasture with the females except in the season of rut, when they are not so wild. As soon as this season is past, however, they fight not only with other beasts but even with those of their own kind.[57]

This seems to be the last wild unicorn sighting in North America, and Dapper's description of them is suspiciously similar to what the Roman naturalist Aelian wrote about unicorns in India 1,500 years previously. However, during the 1700s and 1800s there was a revival of the hope that unicorns may exist somewhere in Africa's unexplored interior or in the kingdoms of Bhutan or Tibet in the remote Asian Himalayas. In the late 1700s a spate of books raised the possibility that unicorns may exist in South Africa. A German explorer, Baron von Wurmb, asserted in 1791 that unicorns "had just been discovered in the interior of Africa." His proof:

Did You Know?

In the 1700s and 1800s some believed that unicorns lived in the kingdoms of Bhutan and Tibet in the Himalayas, and also in South Africa.

What Animals Inspired the Unicorn Stories?

A Boer saw a beast shaped like a horse and with one horn on its brow, ash-gray, and with divided hoofs—his observation went no further. A Hottentot has confirmed this report, and people in these parts quite generally believe in the existence of the unicorn. . . . The future will decide. Various respectable natives have given their servants orders to bring in one of these beasts alive if possible, or else to shoot one, so that we shall soon see the question settled.[58]

A similar willingness to reexamine the unicorn legend in the light of native African reports is found in an 1862 article in the journal *Athenaeum* by William Balfour Baikie, a scientist and African explorer:

The constant belief of the natives of all the countries which I have hitherto visited have partly shaken my skepticism, and at present I simply hold that the non-existence of the unicorn is not proven. A skull of this animal is said to be preserved in the country of Bonú, through which I hope to pass in a few weeks, when I shall make every possible inquiry. Two among my informants have repeatedly declared that they have seen the bones of this animal, and each made a particular mention of the long, straight, or nearly straight, horn.[59]

Far away from Africa, in the Himalaya Mountains, unicorns were said to exist in the remote highlands of Tibet. The *Asiatic*

Journal in 1821 published a letter by Major Latter, a military officer stationed east of Nepal. Latter wrote:

> In a Thibetan manuscript which I procured the other day from the hills, the unicorn is classed under the head of those animals whose hoofs are divided; it is called the one-horned *tso'po.* Upon inquiring what kind of animal it was, to our astonishment the person who brought me the manuscript described exactly the unicorn of the ancients, saying that it was a native of the interior of Thibet, fierce, and extremely wild, seldom ever caught alive, but frequently shot, and that the flesh was used for food. The person who gave me this account has repeatedly seen these animals and eaten flesh of them. They go together in herds, like our wild buffaloes, and are very frequently met with on the borders of the great desert about a month's journey from Lassa.[60]

The same 1821 issue of the *Asiatic Journal* told its readers that "steps have been taken to obtain a complete specimen of the animal supposed to be the unicorn,"[61] but seven years later the journal briefly reported that Latter, after years of futile hunting, was beginning to give up hope. Unfortunately, history does not record any success for the efforts of von Wurmb, Baikie, Latter, or anyone else to document or scientifically demonstrate the existence of unicorns—even though such a demonstration would have undoubtedly brought lasting fame and boundless fortune to anyone who could accomplish the feat.

The standard of proof had changed. Gone were the days when people could cite medieval texts, religious scriptures, ancient Greek or Roman writers, or secondhand accounts to prove that unicorns were real. Scientists led by figures such as Carl Linné (1707–1778) and Comte de Buffon (1707–1788) had helped start a new era of natural history and scientific exploration. This new era, Conniff notes, replaced the "animal folklore that earlier naturalists had complacently repeated since Roman times" with a more rigorous discipline that "demanded specimens and eyewitness accounts."[62] Amateur and professional naturalists explored local environments or, like Charles Darwin, joined expeditionary voyages to observe, paint, preserve, and bottle specimens to be sent back home, scientifically examined, and presented before academic audiences. Today this process continues. Scientists are continually exploring the land and the ocean, using cameras and other recording devices, in an effort to discover and classify species of animals. Using a system of classifying and naming species first developed by Linné in 1758, this army of natural observers has increased the number of known species of life from a few thousand to about 1.7 million. Previously unknown species of large animals have been discovered, including the okapi in 1902, the mountain gorilla that same year, and the komodo dragon in 1910. New species continue to be discovered and classified; as recently as 2007 a new species of leopard was discovered in Borneo.

However, the unicorn has lived up to its reputation by remaining stubbornly elusive in this hunt for scientific knowledge. Sporadic accounts of secondhand sightings continued in the eighteenth, nineteenth, and even twentieth centuries. But there have been no preserved unicorn specimens, no scientifically validated photographs or videos, no authenticated fossils, no peer-reviewed accounts by biologists of unicorns in the wild. Instead, unicorns are mentioned in dwindling numbers of secondhand accounts reporting sightings in evermore remote areas, always said to be just beyond the horizon or the other side of the mountain where the explorer happens to be looking.

For some, the lack of actual proof of the unicorn's existence merely replaces one mystery with another: Namely, if unicorns such as those described by Ctesias or Topsell or the Unicorn Tapestries, did not exist, what inspired so many people to believe in them? One possible answer is that the unicorn was inspired by some other animal. Scientists, unicorn enthusiasts, and others have suggested several possible animals that may have been mistaken for unicorns or could have inspired the unicorn stories.

The Rhinoceros

The rhinoceros is the closest of any of these animals come to the unicorn. While the more familiar rhinos from Africa have two horns, the Indian rhino *(Rhinoceros unicornis)* has just one. Less than 1,000 reside in nature preserves in northern India and Nepal. Less than 300 Javan rhinos, a smaller one-horned species, are scattered in Malaysia and Indonesia.

Technically speaking, rhinos cannot be unicorns because what grows from the rhino's head is not really a horn. The (dual) horns

found on antelopes, goats, and sheep are made of bone, whereas a rhino's horn is made of densely packed keratin, the same substance composing human hair and fingernails. True horns grow through an animal's skin, but a rhinoceros's horn is part of the animal's skin. But from a different and more practical perspective (say, standing in front of a charging rhinoceros), *horn* seems as good a word as any to describe the large and pointed object protruding from the animal's head.

Like the alicorn, rhinoceros horn has long been prized for its medicinal qualities. One reason both African and Indian rhinos are threatened with extinction is that poachers illegally hunt them for their horns. Rhino horn is often ground up and made into medicine in Asian markets, including China and Japan. Writing in 1991, James Cross Giblin notes that "Asian pharmacists in rural areas still prescribe powdered rhino horn as a treatment for snakebite, typhoid fever, headaches, and even insanity."[63] Rhino horn is also touted as a way to restore male virility—sort of an early form of Viagra. Horns are also made into drinking beakers or other tools.

Many of the past descriptions of unicorns sound a lot like the rhinoceros. One notable example comes from Marco Polo (1254–1324). Polo was a trader and explorer who made a historic journey from Venice, Italy, to China and back and wrote a famous book telling of the wonders he witnessed in Asia. On his homeward voyage, on the Indonesian island of Sumatra, he saw a unicorn, or what he thought was a unicorn.

Marco Polo was an Italian trader and explorer who wrote a famous book telling of the wonders he witnessed in Asia. On his homeward voyage, on the Indonesian island of Sumatra, he saw what he thought was a unicorn.

For some, the lack of
actual proof of the
unicorn's existence
merely replaces
one mystery with
another: Namely,
if unicorns such
as those described
by Ctesias or Top-
sell or the Unicorn
Tapestries did not
exist, what inspired
so many people to
believe in them?

Polo wrote:

> There are wild elephants in the country, and
> numerous unicorns, which are nearly as big. They
> have hair like that of a buffalo, feet like those of
> an elephant, and a horn in the middle of the fore-
> head, which is black and very thick. . . . The head
> resembles that of a wild boar, and they carry it
> ever bent towards the ground. They delight much
> to abide in mire and mud. 'Tis a passing ugly beast
> to look upon, and is not in the least like that which
> our stories tell of as being caught in the lap of a
> virgin; in fact, 'tis altogether different from what
> we fancied.[64]

This, many observers conclude, is a pretty good description
of the one-horned Sumatran rhinoceros. (At least one illustrator
of a book of Polo's travels chose to ignore the explorer's written
description of a "passing ugly beast" and instead painted the
familiarly beautiful horselike unicorn.)

Similar older accounts of unicorns can be interpreted as possibly referring to rhinos instead. Ctesias's original and influential description of the Indian "wild ass" with one horn contains
"much rhinoceros in it," argues science writer Willy Ley. He cites
Ctesias's descriptions of the animal's horn and its supposed heal-
ing powers, its surprising swiftness in relation to its lumbering
shape and size (it can run at speeds of up to 40 miles, or 64 ki-
lometers, per hour), and the fact that it is hard to capture. Ley
also finds much rhinoceros in Pliny's description of a monoceros
(one-horn), an animal that "has a stag's head, an elephant's feet,

The Arabian Oryx is a horse-like antelope native to the Arabian Peninsula. They have long, straight, ringed horns that are more than half a yard long. When seen in profile the two horns can appear as one.

and a boar's tail. The rest of the body is like that of a horse. It makes a deep lowing noise, and one black horn two cubits long projects from the middle of the forehead. This animal, they say, cannot be taken alive."[65]

This description might seem strange to modern ears, Ley writes. "We are apt to smile when we read this description nowadays," he argues. "But if compared word for word with a good photograph of an Indian rhinoceros it is not so bad at all. It is the words chosen that make us smile; the facts are not so wrong."[66]

Some people speculate that Pliny's monoceros and other ancient descriptions may derive not from the present-day Indian rhino, but from a species of rhinoceros now extinct. In the early 1900s, fossil bones and skulls of a large rhinoceros-like animal were discovered in Siberia. The extinct species, *Elasmotherium sibericum,* seems to match up well with ancient reports of the

Unicorn Fossils

In 1663 a fossil of a mysterious animal with a 7-foot-long horn (2.3m) was found in a limestone cave near Quedlinburg, Germany. The discovery took place near a mountain where legend told of woman who rode a unicorn. The Quedlinburg fossil was apparently visited—and looted—by many people flocking to the site before it was even excavated (although the horn was not stolen). Eventually a local scientist, Otto von Guericke, was hired to excavate and reconstruct the fossil. He created a strange, two-legged unicorn. This was one of several so-called fossil unicorn discoveries in Europe in the seventeenth and eithteenth centuries. Such evi-

unicorn. It was larger than the present-day Indian rhinoceros, and fossil remains suggest it may well have had a horn situated in the middle of its forehead like a unicorn. But most scientists believe the species probably was already extinct before humans came onto the scene.

dence persuaded some scientists, including the famed mathematician Gottfried Wilhelm Leibniz, to rethink their skepticism about unicorns and accept their existence, at least in

Otto von Guericke's sketch of the unicorn fossil.

the prehistoric past. But most modern scientists who have studied the "unicorn fossils" have concluded that they are really fossilized remains of other prehistoric animals, petrified wood, or natural rock formations.

The Oryx

The Arabian oryx is a horselike antelope native to the Arabian Peninsula. Weighing about 150 pounds (68kg), it has a white coat with brown legs. Both males and females have long, straight, ringed horns that are more than half a yard (45.7cm) long. When seen in profile the two horns can appear as one. The Arab word for "oryx" is *rim*—similar to the *re'em* of Hebrew scripture that has sometimes been translated as "unicorn." The Greek philosopher Aristotle identified the oryx as one of two types of unicorns. All these factors have led some to wonder whether the oryx inspired the unicorn legend. Vincenzo Maria, a friar of the Carmelite order, saw oryxes on display and wrote in 1656 that they were "as large as stags, similar to them in shape but . . . they are the purest white. . . . I myself believe these creatures to be those which some writers describe as the Unicorn."[67]

Like the rhinoceros—and the unicorn—the oryx has been hunted down for its horns, believed to have great medinical value. The Arabian oryx became extinct in the wild in 1972. Zoos such as the San Diego Wild Animal Park saved the species from total extinction through a captive breeding program, and small wild populations have been reintroduced in the Persian Gulf region.

The Chiru

Another prime candidate for unicorn inspiration is the Tibetan antelope, also known as the chiru or the orongo. It inhabits the sparsely populated Tibetan plateau at elevations between 13,000 and 18,000 feet (4km and 5.5km), grows to 4 feet (1.2m) in height, and has a gray to reddish-brown coat. Its horns, which grow on the male only, are about 2 feet (0.6m) long, straight, and heavily ridged—and perhaps may look like one horn when seen in profile. Writer James Cross Giblin suggests that Ctesias, the Greek chronicler who wrote of the unicorn in India but had never been to India himself, may have mixed up descriptions of the chiru and the Indian rhinoceros. "As accounts of these animals were passed on from trader to merchant to people like Ctesias, their traits probably became combined."[68]

According to an account by Lieu-tenant Colonel N. Prejevalsky, the author of a book on Mongolia and Tibet published in 1876, the native Mongolians attached religious sig-nificance to the orongo and its horn. "Mongols tell fortunes and predict future events by the rings on these [horns]; and they also serve to mark out the burial places ... of deceased lamas [Buddhist monks]," wrote Prejevalsky. Prejevalsky goes on to write that the antelope horns "are carried away in large numbers by pilgrims returning from Thibet and are sold at high prices. Mongols tell you that a whip-handle made out of one will prevent a rider's steed from tiring. Another prevalent supersti-tion is that the orongo has only one horn growing vertically from the centre of its head."[69]

Some unicorn researchers specu-late that although people who lived close to the chiru or orongo knew that the animal had in fact two horns, as the horns themselves became articles of trade and spread to further regions, people came to believe that they actually came from a one-horned ani-mal. Shepard writes:

Georges Leopold Cuvier argued that a uni-corn-like horn sprouting from the middle of the forehead was impossible because of divi-sions in the frontal skull bone right at the spot where a unicorn's horn would have grown.

"It's a goat."

—A girl says when
viewing a goat whose
horns had been
manipulated into
one horn to look like
a unicorn for a
circus show.

The priests who use the horns in divination may know that they grew in pairs, although they use them singly, but the pilgrims who buy these horns and carry them into the surrounding districts are probably not aware of this. At a distance from the distributing centre everyone is convinced that they are the horns of unicorns. . . . Tibet was included in the "India" of Ctesias.—Why should we look farther for the sources of the unicorn?[7]

Sadly, the chiru shares with its unicorn brothers an uncertain fate due to human hunting. In this case, the prize is not its horn, but its *shatoosh*—extremely soft and fine wool—which can only be obtained by killing the animal. Its numbers have dropped from nearly 1 million (estimated) at the turn of the twentieth century to fewer than 75,000 today.

Artificial Unicorns

Another possibility is that unicorn stories may have been inspired by experiments with animal breeding and raising. Some of these experiments may have produced one-horned animals by inducing the growth of a single horn in a cow, goat, or antelope. In the 1930s, a biologist and doctor in Maine named W. Franklin Dove developed an interest in unicorns. Dove observed in a 1936 article:

That the unicorn can be produced artificially has been suggested a number of times in the past. Le Vaillant, 1796, in his "Travels in Africa," describes a process of manipulating the horns of oxen. "As the horns of the young ox sprout they are trained over

Unicorn tales have been around for thousands of years and will continue to be as no one has proven that they do not exist.

the forehead until the points meet. They are then manipulated so as to make them coalesce, and so shoot upwards from the middle of the forehead, like the horn of the fabled unicorn.[71]

Similar stories could also be found in in the writings of the Roman natural historian Pliny. Much later accounts, dating to the early twentith century, describe how rams in Nepal were branded on their heads to induce unicorn-like horns (such rams were exhibited in London in 1906). Other accounts tell of the Dinka people in southern Sudan who, Dove wrote, apparently manipulated horns on their cattle to create single-horn specicmens "as a means of marking the leaders of their herds."[72]

Dove also noted that most European and American scientists doubted the abilities of shepherds in Nepal or cattle herders in Africa to create one-horned animals. Their skepticism seem confirmed by the French naturalist Georges Leopold Cuvier, who published his findings in 1827. Cuvier had studied goats, sheep, and other animals with cloven or divided hoofs (the unicorn was usually portrayed as having such hoofs). He found that all such animals had divisions in the frontal skull bone as well—right at the spot where a unicorn's horn would have grown. Cuvier argued that such horns had to grow out from the skull, not from its division. Thus a unicorn-like horn sprouting from the middle of the forehead was impossible. But Dove's own research into cows had led him to conclude their horns were not outgrowths of the skull, but instead stemmed from horn buds "residing in tissues above the frontal bones" that later took root in the skull. Thus, he thought, "the opportunity was available to study the ability of these tissues, when brought closely together, to fuse."[73]

A Scientist Creates a Unicorn

In March 1933, Dove performed his experiment. He cut open the scalp of a bull calf and transplanted its horn buds from the side to the center of its skull, placing them close together. The two horn buds did in fact fuse and produce a single horn growing from the center of the bull's forehead. "The animal, now two and a half years old," Dove wrote in 1936, "bears upon the forehead the stamp of the once fabulous unicorn."[74] Dove's operation was relatively simple, leading some to believe that similar operations may well have been done in Nepal, Africa, and other places to create single-horned creatures.

Some other fascinating details, in addition to the horn itself, matched descriptions in unicorn lore. The breed of cattle that this calf belonged to usually had curved horns, but this single horn was straight with only a slight curve at its tip. Ctesias had claimed that unicorn horns were multicolored, being white at the base, black in the middle, and red at the tip. Dove observed that the horn of his unicorn was "white or grayish-white at the base and is tipped with black" and that a female of that breed would have had a red-tipped horn "since color appears as a sex-limited factor in this particular breed." Perhaps even more interestingly, according to Dove his one-horned bull exhibited some of the same behaviors associated with unicorns. "He recognizes the power of a single horn which he uses as a prow to pass under fences and barriers in his path, or as a forward thrusting bayonet in his attacks. . . . [But] his ability to inherit the earth gives him the virtues of meekness. Consciousness of power makes him docile."[75] In other words, Dove's calf was powerful, yet gentle and humble, like a unicorn was supposed to be.

Unicorns at the Circus

In 1985 an interesting replication of Dove's experiment was featured at "The Greatest Show on Earth," also known as the Ringling Brothers and Barnum and Bailey Circus. "Children of all ages, an event unparalleled in history—the Living Unicorn!" boomed the announcer as a glittering procession marched into Madison Square Garden. On a golden float, accompanied by an attractive young woman, stood a snowy-white creature with a long, single horn. A *Newsweek* article quotes a 10-year-old girl's pronouncement on the creature: "It's a goat."[76]

She was right. The animal was one of four angora goats the circus had bought from a California couple, Otter G'Zell and Morning Glory, who had transplanted horn buds to create the single horn. They claimed that unicorns were not mere myth or a particular species, but a lost art they had rediscovered. Animal rights activists protested, arguing that it was cruel to alter or mutilate animals for public display. Stung by bad publicity, the circus soon retired its "Living Unicorn." One of the unicorns/ goats came back into the public eye in 2006 when it, or rather its stuffed and preserved remains, went on display at the Palace of Wonders, a sideshow-themed bar in Washington, D.C. Perhaps one could go see it to this day, but the setting—on display with a fur-covered trout, a five-legged dog, and a collection of shrunken heads—might be disheartening to some exploring the unicorn mystery today.

Does it matter whether or not unicorns did exist in some form or other, or if the unicorn myth grew from ancient mistakes and misidentifications of the rhinoceros? Would the Unicorn Tapestries be any less wondrous if unicorns were entirely imaginary? Is the spirit of the unicorn to be found in Dove's calf, or in fantasy books such as *The Last Unicorn* by Peter S. Beagle? Perhaps the final word should go to the German poet Rainer Maria Rilke and his meditation on unicorns and the role that artists, storytellers, and dreamers have on the unicorn's existence, and our own.

Oh, this is the animal that doesn't exist.
They didn't know that, and in any case—
Its neck, its bearing, its stride,
And the light of its calm gaze—they have loved.

In fact, it never was. But since they loved it,
A pure animal came to be.

They always left enough space.
And in that space, clear and unlocked,
It freely raised its head and did not
Need to be. They nourished him not with grain,
But always with the possibility to be.

And they gave the animal such a power
That from its forehead a horn grew. One horn.
To a maiden he came thereby, all-white
And was inside the mirror-silver, and in her.[77]

Perhaps the unicorn has just as much reality as our human imagination can endow it with. Or perhaps the unicorn has just a little bit more.

NOTES

Introduction Wrapped in Mystery

1. C.S. Lewis, *The Last Battle*. New York: Collier, 1970, pp. 87–88.

Chapter 1: Ancient Stories and Images

2. Nancy Hathaway, *The Unicorn*. New York: Avenel, 1980, p. 164.
3. Odell Shepard, *The Lore of the Unicorn*. New York: Avenel, 1982, p. 97.
4. Shepard, *The Lore of the Unicorn*, p. 96.
5. James Cross Giblin, *The Truth About Unicorns*. New York: HarperCollins, 1991, p. 39.
6. Matti Megged, *The Animal That Never Was*. New York: Lumen, 1992, pp. 27–28.
7. Rüdiger Robert Beer, *Unicorn: Myth and Reality*. New York: Van Nostrand Reinhold, 1972, pp. 69–70.
8. Quoted in Welleran Poltarnees, *A Book of Unicorns*. La Jolla, CA: Green Tiger, 1978, p. 6.
9. Quoted in Margaret B. Freeman, *The Unicorn Tapestries*. New York: Metropolitan Museum of Art, 1976, p. 14.
10. Quoted in Freeman, *The Unicorn Tapestries*, p. 14.
11. Quoted in Shepard, *The Lore of the Unicorn*, p. 37.
12. Quoted in Poltarnees, *A Book of Unicorns*, p. 7.
13. Quoted in Freeman, *The Unicorn Tapestries*, p. 19.
14. Shepard, *The Lore of the Unicorn*, p. 47.
15. Freeman, *The Unicorn Tapestries*, p. 19.

Chapter 2: The Unicorn in Medieval Times

16. Hathaway, *The Unicorn*, p. 13.
17. Quoted in Freeman, *The Unicorn Tapestries*, p. 17.
18. Quoted in Freeman, *The Unicorn Tapestries*, p. 17.
19. John Williamson, *The Oak King, the Holly King, and the Unicorn: The Myths and Symbolism of the Unicorn Tapestries*. New York: Harper & Row, 1986, p. 49.
20. Quoted in Freeman, *The Unicorn Tapestries*, p. 19.
21. Giblin, *The Truth About Unicorns*, p. 45.
22. Beer, *Unicorn*, p. 47.
23. Megged, *The Animal That Never Was*, p. 28.
24. Shepard, *The Lore of the Unicorn*, pp. 73–74.
25. Shepard, *The Lore of the Unicorn*, p. 76.
26. Quoted in Georgess McHargue, *The Beasts of Never*. New York: Delacorte, 1987, p.75.

Chapter 3: Hunting the Unicorn

27. Quoted in Shepard, *The Lore of the Unicorn*, p. 192.
28. Shepard, *The Lore of the Unicorn*, pp. 192–193.
29. Giblin, *The Truth About Unicorns*, p. 59.
30. Quoted in Giblin, *The Truth About Unicorns*, p. 49.
31. Quoted in Maria Tatar, ed., *The Annotated Brothers Grimm*. New York: Norton, 2004, p. 109.

32. Edward Topsell, *The Elizabethan Zoo: A Book of Beasts Both Fabulous and Authentic.* Boston: Nonpareil, 1979, p. 91.
33. Quoted in Joseph Nigg, ed., *The Book of Fabulous Beasts.* New York: Oxford University Press, 1999, p. 181.
34. Shepard, *The Lore of the Unicorn,* p. 244.
35. McHargue, *The Beasts of Never,* p. 66.
36. Robert Vavra, *Unicorns I Have Known.* New York: William Morrow, 1983, p. 140.
37. Vavra, *Unicorns I Have Known,* p. 199.
38. Quoted in Jess Tierney, "He's Hung with Hemingway and Chased After Unicorns," *College Hill Independent.* www.brown.edu.

Chapter 4: The Unicorn's Magic Horn

39. Quoted in Poltarnees, *A Book of Unicorns,* p. 23.
40. Shepard, *The Lore of the Unicorn,* p. 119.
41. Quoted in Fred Bruemmer, *The Narwhal: Unicorn of the Sea.* Toronto: Key Porter, 1993, p. 53.
42. Quoted in Shepard, *The Lore of the Unicorn,* p. 27.
43. Giblin, *The Truth About Unicorns,* p. 12.
44. Shepard, *The Lore of the Unicorn,* p. 123.
45. Shepard, *The Lore of the Unicorn,* p. 124.
46. Quoted in Shepard, *The Lore of the Unicorn,* p. 29.
47. Quoted in Hathaway, *The Unicorn,* p. 115.
48. Quoted in Noel D. Vietmeyer, "Rare Narwhals Inspired the Myth of the Unicorn," *Smithsonian,* February 1980, p.118.
49. Quoted in Vietmeyer, p. 119.
50. Quoted in Bruemmer, *The Narwhal,* p. 55.
51. Bruemmer, *The Narwhal,* p. 12.
52. Bruemmer, *The Narwhal,* p. 12.
53. Quoted in Giblin, *The Truth About Unicorns,* pp. 83–84.
54. Quoted in Bruemmer, *The Narwhal,* p. 120.
55. Quoted in William Jackson, "The Use of Unicorn Horn in Medicine," *Pharmaceutical Journal,* December 2004, p. 927.

Chapter 5: What Animals Inspired the Unicorn Stories?

56. Richard Conniff, "Happy Birthday, Linnaeus," *Natural History,* December 2006/January 2007, p. 43.
57. Quoted in Poltarnees, *The Book of Unicorns,* p. 8.
58. Quoted in Shepard, *The Lore of the Unicorn,* p. 204.
59. Quoted in Shepard, *The Lore of the Unicorn,* p. 205.
60. Quoted in Shepard, *The Lore of the Unicorn,* p. 210.
61. Quoted in Shepard, *The Lore of the Unicorn,* p. 210.
62. Conniff, "Happy Birthday, Linnaeus," p. 43.
63. Giblin, *The Truth About Unicorns,* p. 97.
64. Quoted in Joe Nigg, *Wonder Beasts: Tales and Lore of the Phoenix, the Griffin, the Unicorn, and the Dragon.* Englewood, CO: Libraries Unlimited, 1995, p. 81.
65. Quoted in Willy Ley, *The Lungfish, the Dodo, and the Unicorn: An Excursion into Romantic Zoology.* New York: Viking, 1948, p. 26.
66. Ley, *The Lungfish, the Dodo, and the Unicorn,* p. 26.
67. Quoted in Bruemmer, *The Narwhal,* p. 20.
68. Giblin, *The Truth About Unicorns,* p. 10.
69. Quoted in Shepard, *The Lore of the Unicorn,* p. 211.
70. Shepard, *The Lore of the Unicorn,* p. 226.
71. W. Franklin Dove, "Artificial Production of the

Fabulous Unicorn: A Modern Interpretation of an Ancient Myth." *Scientific Monthly,* May 1936, p. 432.

72. Quoted in Dove, "Artificial Production of the Fabulous Unicorn," p. 433.

73. Dove, "Artificial Production of the Fabulous Unicorn," p. 434.

74. Dove, "Artificial Production of the Fabulous Unicorn," p. 435.

75. Dove, "Artificial Production of the Fabulous Unicorn," p. 435.

76. Quoted in *Newsweek,* "A Unicorn—or a Goat?" April 22, 1985, p. 32.

77. Quoted in Megged, *The Animal That Never Was,* p. 1.

FOR FURTHER RESEARCH

Books

Fred Bruemmer, *The Narwhal: Unicorn of the Sea.* Toronto: Key Porter, 1993. An informative and well-illustrated book on both the mythical unicorn and the real narwhal.

Adolfo Salvatore Cavallo, *The Unicorn Tapestries at the Metropolitan Museum of Art.* New York: Abrams, 1998. An examination of the famous tapestries that incorporates recent scholarship of their creation and meaning.

Bruce Coville, *The Unicorn Treasury: Stories, Poems, and Unicorn Lore.* Orlando, FL: Magic Carpet, 2004. An anthology of poems, stories, and essays about unicorns.

John Hamilton, *Unicorns and Other Magical Creatures.* Edina, MN: ABDO, 2005. An overview of unicorns in ancient myth and contemporary fantasy for younger readers.

Nancy Hathaway, *The Unicorn.* New York: Avenel, 1984. A handsomely illustrated book for unicorn lovers that includes retellings of unicorn tales and historical information on unicorn accounts and art.

Patricia D. Netzley, *Unicorns.* San Diego: Lucent, 2001. A basic introduction to the unicorn and its role in religion and medicine, as well as efforts to determine its existence.

Lucille Recht Penner, *Unicorns.* New York: Random House, 2005. For very young readers.

Welleran Poltarnees, *A Book of Unicorns.* La Jolla, CA: Green Tiger, 1978. An unmatched collection of primary sources and artwork on the unicorn.

Odell Shepard, *The Lore of the Unicorn.* New York: Avenel, 1982. Originally published in 1930, this is still considered a definitive study of the unicorn.

Web Sites

All About Unicorns (www.allaboutunicorns. com). The Web site features information on unicorns and pictures of unicorns of all types.

The Medieval Bestiary (http://bestiary.ca). An online repository of information on bestiaries, including numerous texts. Includes a subject search tool for looking for writings on the unicorn.

Mystical Unicorn by the Unicorn Lady (www.unicornlady.net). A personal multimedia guide to unicorn lore.

Narwhal Tusk Discoveries (www.narwhal. org). A comprehensive Web site on the narwhal, including current research and historical information on the alicorn trade.

The Unicorn Tapestries (www.metmuseum. org/explore/Unicorn/unicorn_splash.htm). Part of the "Explore and Learn" section of the Metropolitan Museum of Art's Web site; it features images and information on the famous Unicorn Tapestries.

INDEX

ABOUT THE AUTHOR

William Dudley has edited and written numerous anthologies on social and historical topics. He lives in San Diego with his wife, children, cat, and turtles. He has traveled to many places, including China, Tibet, India, and Germany, but has never seen a unicorn.